THIS IS YOUR **PASSBOOK**® FOR ...

DEVELOPMENTAL DISABILITIES PROGRAM AIDE

NATIONAL LEARNING CORPORATION®
passbooks.com

COPYRIGHT NOTICE

Copyright © 2018 by

National Learning Corporation

212 Michael Drive, Syosset, NY 11791
(516) 921-8888 • www.passbooks.com
E-mail: info@passbooks.com

PUBLISHED IN THE UNITED STATES OF AMERICA

PASSBOOK® SERIES

THE *PASSBOOK® SERIES* has been created to prepare applicants and candidates for the ultimate academic battlefield – the examination room.

At some time in our lives, each and every one of us may be required to take an examination – for validation, matriculation, admission, qualification, registration, certification, or licensure.

Based on the assumption that every applicant or candidate has met the basic formal educational standards, has taken the required number of courses, and read the necessary texts, the *PASSBOOK® SERIES* furnishes the one special preparation which may assure passing with confidence, instead of failing with insecurity. Examination questions – together with answers – are furnished as the basic vehicle for study so that the mysteries of the examination and its compounding difficulties may be eliminated or diminished by a sure method.

This book is meant to help you pass your examination provided that you qualify and are serious in your objective.

The entire field is reviewed through the huge store of content information which is succinctly presented through a provocative and challenging approach – the question-and-answer method.

A climate of success is established by furnishing the correct answers at the end of each test.

You soon learn to recognize types of questions, forms of questions, and patterns of questioning. You may even begin to anticipate expected outcomes.

You perceive that many questions are repeated or adapted so that you can gain acute insights, which may enable you to score many sure points.

You learn how to confront new questions, or types of questions, and to attack them confidently and work out the correct answers.

You note objectives and emphases, and recognize pitfalls and dangers, so that you may make positive educational adjustments.

Moreover, you are kept fully informed in relation to new concepts, methods, practices, and directions in the field.

You discover that you arre actually taking the examination all the time: you are preparing for the examination by "taking" an examination, not by reading extraneous and/or supererogatory textbooks.

In short, this PASSBOOK®, used directedly, should be an important factor in helping you to pass your test.

DEVELOPMENTAL DISABILITIES SECURE CARE TREATMENT AIDE

DUTIES
As a Developmental Disabilities Secure Care Treatment Aide, you would assist in the treatment and care of mentally retarded/developmentally disabled persons who are highly assaultive, suicidal or dangerous to themselves or others within a designated secure facility. You would be responsible for providing a safe, secure, stable environment within which these severely disturbed and agitated patients can be given the intensive care needed for stabilization and treatment.

SUBJECT OF EXAMINATION
The written test will be designed to test for knowledge, skills, and/or abilities in such areas as:
1. Dealing with daily situations in an OMRDD secure care setting;
2. Observing and recording situations of daily living;
3. Understanding and applying written instructional material; and
4. Arithmetic for daily living.

HOW TO TAKE A TEST

I. YOU MUST PASS AN EXAMINATION

A. *WHAT EVERY CANDIDATE SHOULD KNOW*

Examination applicants often ask us for help in preparing for the written test. What can I study in advance? What kinds of questions will be asked? How will the test be given? How will the papers be graded?

As an applicant for a civil service examination, you may be wondering about some of these things. Our purpose here is to suggest effective methods of advance study and to describe civil service examinations.

Your chances for success on this examination can be increased if you know how to prepare. Those "pre-examination jitters" can be reduced if you know what to expect. You can even experience an adventure in good citizenship if you know why civil service exams are given.

B. *WHY ARE CIVIL SERVICE EXAMINATIONS GIVEN?*

Civil service examinations are important to you in two ways. As a citizen, you want public jobs filled by employees who know how to do their work. As a job seeker, you want a fair chance to compete for that job on an equal footing with other candidates. The best-known means of accomplishing this two-fold goal is the competitive examination.

Exams are widely publicized throughout the nation. They may be administered for jobs in federal, state, city, municipal, town or village governments or agencies.

Any citizen may apply, with some limitations, such as the age or residence of applicants. Your experience and education may be reviewed to see whether you meet the requirements for the particular examination. When these requirements exist, they are reasonable and applied consistently to all applicants. Thus, a competitive examination may cause you some uneasiness now, but it is your privilege and safeguard.

C. *HOW ARE CIVIL SERVICE EXAMS DEVELOPED?*

Examinations are carefully written by trained technicians who are specialists in the field known as "psychological measurement," in consultation with recognized authorities in the field of work that the test will cover. These experts recommend the subject matter areas or skills to be tested; only those knowledges or skills important to your success on the job are included. The most reliable books and source materials available are used as references. Together, the experts and technicians judge the difficulty level of the questions.

Test technicians know how to phrase questions so that the problem is clearly stated. Their ethics do not permit "trick" or "catch" questions. Questions may have been tried out on sample groups, or subjected to statistical analysis, to determine their usefulness.

Written tests are often used in combination with performance tests, ratings of training and experience, and oral interviews. All of these measures combine to form the best-known means of finding the right person for the right job.

II. HOW TO PASS THE WRITTEN TEST

A. NATURE OF THE EXAMINATION

To prepare intelligently for civil service examinations, you should know how they differ from school examinations you have taken. In school you were assigned certain definite pages to read or subjects to cover. The examination questions were quite detailed and usually emphasized memory. Civil service exams, on the other hand, try to discover your present ability to perform the duties of a position, plus your potentiality to learn these duties. In other words, a civil service exam attempts to predict how successful you will be. Questions cover such a broad area that they cannot be as minute and detailed as school exam questions.

In the public service similar kinds of work, or positions, are grouped together in one "class." This process is known as *position-classification.* All the positions in a class are paid according to the salary range for that class. One class title covers all of these positions, and they are all tested by the same examination.

B. FOUR BASIC STEPS

1) Study the announcement

How, then, can you know what subjects to study? Our best answer is: "Learn as much as possible about the class of positions for which you've applied." The exam will test the knowledge, skills and abilities needed to do the work.

Your most valuable source of information about the position you want is the official exam announcement. This announcement lists the training and experience qualifications. Check these standards and apply only if you come reasonably close to meeting them.

The brief description of the position in the examination announcement offers some clues to the subjects which will be tested. Think about the job itself. Review the duties in your mind. Can you perform them, or are there some in which you are rusty? Fill in the blank spots in your preparation.

Many jurisdictions preview the written test in the exam announcement by including a section called "Knowledge and Abilities Required," "Scope of the Examination," or some similar heading. Here you will find out specifically what fields will be tested.

2) Review your own background

Once you learn in general what the position is all about, and what you need to know to do the work, ask yourself which subjects you already know fairly well and which need improvement. You may wonder whether to concentrate on improving your strong areas or on building some background in your fields of weakness. When the announcement has specified "some knowledge" or "considerable knowledge," or has used adjectives like "beginning principles of…" or "advanced … methods," you can get a clue as to the number and difficulty of questions to be asked in any given field. More questions, and hence broader coverage, would be included for those subjects which are more important in the work. Now weigh your strengths and weaknesses against the job requirements and prepare accordingly.

3) Determine the level of the position

Another way to tell how intensively you should prepare is to understand the level of the job for which you are applying. Is it the entering level? In other words, is this the position in which beginners in a field of work are hired? Or is it an intermediate or advanced level? Sometimes this is indicated by such words as "Junior" or "Senior" in the class title. Other jurisdictions use Roman numerals to designate the level – Clerk I, Clerk II, for example. The word "Supervisor" sometimes appears in the title. If the level is not indicated by the title, check the description of duties. Will you be working under very close supervision, or will you have responsibility for independent decisions in this work?

4) Choose appropriate study materials

Now that you know the subjects to be examined and the relative amount of each subject to be covered, you can choose suitable study materials. For beginning level jobs, or even advanced ones, if you have a pronounced weakness in some aspect of your training, read a modern, standard textbook in that field. Be sure it is up to date and has general coverage. Such books are normally available at your library, and the librarian will be glad to help you locate one. For entry-level positions, questions of appropriate difficulty are chosen – neither highly advanced questions, nor those too simple. Such questions require careful thought but not advanced training.

If the position for which you are applying is technical or advanced, you will read more advanced, specialized material. If you are already familiar with the basic principles of your field, elementary textbooks would waste your time. Concentrate on advanced textbooks and technical periodicals. Think through the concepts and review difficult problems in your field.

These are all general sources. You can get more ideas on your own initiative, following these leads. For example, training manuals and publications of the government agency which employs workers in your field can be useful, particularly for technical and professional positions. A letter or visit to the government department involved may result in more specific study suggestions, and certainly will provide you with a more definite idea of the exact nature of the position you are seeking.

III. KINDS OF TESTS

Tests are used for purposes other than measuring knowledge and ability to perform specified duties. For some positions, it is equally important to test ability to make adjustments to new situations or to profit from training. In others, basic mental abilities not dependent on information are essential. Questions which test these things may not appear as pertinent to the duties of the position as those which test for knowledge and information. Yet they are often highly important parts of a fair examination. For very general questions, it is almost impossible to help you direct your study efforts. What we can do is to point out some of the more common of these general abilities needed in public service positions and describe some typical questions.

1) General information

Broad, general information has been found useful for predicting job success in some kinds of work. This is tested in a variety of ways, from vocabulary lists to questions about current events. Basic background in some field of work, such as sociology or economics, may be sampled in a group of questions. Often these are principles which have become familiar to most persons through exposure rather than through formal training. It is difficult to advise you how to study for these questions; being alert to the world around you is our best suggestion.

2) Verbal ability

An example of an ability needed in many positions is verbal or language ability. Verbal ability is, in brief, the ability to use and understand words. Vocabulary and grammar tests are typical measures of this ability. Reading comprehension or paragraph interpretation questions are common in many kinds of civil service tests. You are given a paragraph of written material and asked to find its central meaning.

3) Numerical ability

Number skills can be tested by the familiar arithmetic problem, by checking paired lists of numbers to see which are alike and which are different, or by interpreting charts and graphs. In the latter test, a graph may be printed in the test booklet which you are asked to use as the basis for answering questions.

4) Observation

A popular test for law-enforcement positions is the observation test. A picture is shown to you for several minutes, then taken away. Questions about the picture test your ability to observe both details and larger elements.

5) Following directions

In many positions in the public service, the employee must be able to carry out written instructions dependably and accurately. You may be given a chart with several columns, each column listing a variety of information. The questions require you to carry out directions involving the information given in the chart.

6) Skills and aptitudes

Performance tests effectively measure some manual skills and aptitudes. When the skill is one in which you are trained, such as typing or shorthand, you can practice. These tests are often very much like those given in business school or high school courses. For many of the other skills and aptitudes, however, no short-time preparation can be made. Skills and abilities natural to you or that you have developed throughout your lifetime are being tested.

Many of the general questions just described provide all the data needed to answer the questions and ask you to use your reasoning ability to find the answers. Your best preparation for these tests, as well as for tests of facts and ideas, is to be at your physical and mental best. You, no doubt, have your own methods of getting into an exam-taking mood and keeping "in shape." The next section lists some ideas on this subject.

IV. KINDS OF QUESTIONS

Only rarely is the "essay" question, which you answer in narrative form, used in civil service tests. Civil service tests are usually of the short-answer type. Full instructions for answering these questions will be given to you at the examination. But in case this is your first experience with short-answer questions and separate answer sheets, here is what you need to know:

1) Multiple-choice Questions

Most popular of the short-answer questions is the "multiple choice" or "best answer" question. It can be used, for example, to test for factual knowledge, ability to solve problems or judgment in meeting situations found at work.

A multiple-choice question is normally one of three types—

- It can begin with an incomplete statement followed by several possible endings. You are to find the one ending which *best* completes the statement, although some of the others may not be entirely wrong.
- It can also be a complete statement in the form of a question which is answered by choosing one of the statements listed.
- It can be in the form of a problem – again you select the best answer.

Here is an example of a multiple-choice question with a discussion which should give you some clues as to the method for choosing the right answer:

When an employee has a complaint about his assignment, the action which will *best* help him overcome his difficulty is to
  - A. discuss his difficulty with his coworkers
  - B. take the problem to the head of the organization
  - C. take the problem to the person who gave him the assignment
  - D. say nothing to anyone about his complaint

In answering this question, you should study each of the choices to find which is best. Consider choice "A" – Certainly an employee may discuss his complaint with fellow employees, but no change or improvement can result, and the complaint remains unresolved. Choice "B" is a poor choice since the head of the organization probably does not know what assignment you have been given, and taking your problem to him is known as "going over the head" of the supervisor. The supervisor, or person who made the assignment, is the person who can clarify it or correct any injustice. Choice "C" is, therefore, correct. To say nothing, as in choice "D," is unwise. Supervisors have and interest in knowing the problems employees are facing, and the employee is seeking a solution to his problem.

2) True/False Questions

The "true/false" or "right/wrong" form of question is sometimes used. Here a complete statement is given. Your job is to decide whether the statement is right or wrong.

SAMPLE: A roaming cell-phone call to a nearby city costs less than a non-roaming call to a distant city.

This statement is wrong, or false, since roaming calls are more expensive.

This is not a complete list of all possible question forms, although most of the others are variations of these common types. You will always get complete directions for answering questions. Be sure you understand *how* to mark your answers – ask questions until you do.

V. RECORDING YOUR ANSWERS

Computer terminals are used more and more today for many different kinds of exams.

For an examination with very few applicants, you may be told to record your answers in the test booklet itself. Separate answer sheets are much more common. If this separate answer sheet is to be scored by machine – and this is often the case – it is highly important that you mark your answers correctly in order to get credit.

An electronic scoring machine is often used in civil service offices because of the speed with which papers can be scored. Machine-scored answer sheets must be marked with a pencil, which will be given to you. This pencil has a high graphite content which responds to the electronic scoring machine. As a matter of fact, stray dots may register as answers, so do not let your pencil rest on the answer sheet while you are pondering the correct answer. Also, if your pencil lead breaks or is otherwise defective, ask for another.

Since the answer sheet will be dropped in a slot in the scoring machine, be careful not to bend the corners or get the paper crumpled.

The answer sheet normally has five vertical columns of numbers, with 30 numbers to a column. These numbers correspond to the question numbers in your test booklet. After each number, going across the page are four or five pairs of dotted lines. These short dotted lines have small letters or numbers above them. The first two pairs may also have a "T" or "F" above the letters. This indicates that the first two pairs only are to be used if the questions are of the true-false type. If the questions are multiple choice, disregard the "T" and "F" and pay attention only to the small letters or numbers.

Answer your questions in the manner of the sample that follows:

32. The largest city in the United States is
    A. Washington, D.C.
    B. New York City
    C. Chicago
    D. Detroit
    E. San Francisco

1) Choose the answer you think is best. (New York City is the largest, so "B" is correct.)
2) Find the row of dotted lines numbered the same as the question you are answering. (Find row number 32)
3) Find the pair of dotted lines corresponding to the answer. (Find the pair of lines under the mark "B.")
4) Make a solid black mark between the dotted lines.

VI. BEFORE THE TEST

Common sense will help you find procedures to follow to get ready for an examination. Too many of us, however, overlook these sensible measures. Indeed, nervousness and fatigue have been found to be the most serious reasons why applicants fail to do their best on civil service tests. Here is a list of reminders:

- Begin your preparation early – Don't wait until the last minute to go scurrying around for books and materials or to find out what the position is all about.
- Prepare continuously – An hour a night for a week is better than an all-night cram session. This has been definitely established. What is more, a night a week for a month will return better dividends than crowding your study into a shorter period of time.
- Locate the place of the exam – You have been sent a notice telling you when and where to report for the examination. If the location is in a different town or otherwise unfamiliar to you, it would be well to inquire the best route and learn something about the building.
- Relax the night before the test – Allow your mind to rest. Do not study at all that night. Plan some mild recreation or diversion; then go to bed early and get a good night's sleep.
- Get up early enough to make a leisurely trip to the place for the test – This way unforeseen events, traffic snarls, unfamiliar buildings, etc. will not upset you.
- Dress comfortably – A written test is not a fashion show. You will be known by number and not by name, so wear something comfortable.
- Leave excess paraphernalia at home – Shopping bags and odd bundles will get in your way. You need bring only the items mentioned in the official notice you received; usually everything you need is provided. Do not bring reference books to the exam. They will only confuse those last minutes and be taken away from you when in the test room.
- Arrive somewhat ahead of time – If because of transportation schedules you must get there very early, bring a newspaper or magazine to take your mind off yourself while waiting.
- Locate the examination room – When you have found the proper room, you will be directed to the seat or part of the room where you will sit. Sometimes you are given a sheet of instructions to read while you are waiting. Do not fill out any forms until you are told to do so; just read them and be prepared.
- Relax and prepare to listen to the instructions
- If you have any physical problem that may keep you from doing your best, be sure to tell the test administrator. If you are sick or in poor health, you really cannot do your best on the exam. You can come back and take the test some other time.

VII. AT THE TEST

The day of the test is here and you have the test booklet in your hand. The temptation to get going is very strong. Caution! There is more to success than knowing the right answers. You must know how to identify your papers and understand variations in the type of short-answer question used in this particular examination. Follow these suggestions for maximum results from your efforts:

1) Cooperate with the monitor

The test administrator has a duty to create a situation in which you can be as much at ease as possible. He will give instructions, tell you when to begin, check to see that you are marking your answer sheet correctly, and so on. He is not there to guard you, although he will see that your competitors do not take unfair advantage. He wants to help you do your best.

2) Listen to all instructions

Don't jump the gun! Wait until you understand all directions. In most civil service tests you get more time than you need to answer the questions. So don't be in a hurry. Read each word of instructions until you clearly understand the meaning. Study the examples, listen to all announcements and follow directions. Ask questions if you do not understand what to do.

3) Identify your papers

Civil service exams are usually identified by number only. You will be assigned a number; you must not put your name on your test papers. Be sure to copy your number correctly. Since more than one exam may be given, copy your exact examination title.

4) Plan your time

Unless you are told that a test is a "speed" or "rate of work" test, speed itself is usually not important. Time enough to answer all the questions will be provided, but this does not mean that you have all day. An overall time limit has been set. Divide the total time (in minutes) by the number of questions to determine the approximate time you have for each question.

5) Do not linger over difficult questions

If you come across a difficult question, mark it with a paper clip (useful to have along) and come back to it when you have been through the booklet. One caution if you do this – be sure to skip a number on your answer sheet as well. Check often to be sure that you have not lost your place and that you are marking in the row numbered the same as the question you are answering.

6) Read the questions

Be sure you know what the question asks! Many capable people are unsuccessful because they failed to *read* the questions correctly.

7) Answer all questions

Unless you have been instructed that a penalty will be deducted for incorrect answers, it is better to guess than to omit a question.

8) Speed tests

It is often better NOT to guess on speed tests. It has been found that on timed tests people are tempted to spend the last few seconds before time is called in marking answers at random – without even reading them – in the hope of picking up a few extra points. To discourage this practice, the instructions may warn you that your score will be "corrected" for guessing. That is, a penalty will be applied. The incorrect answers will be deducted from the correct ones, or some other penalty formula will be used.

9) Review your answers

If you finish before time is called, go back to the questions you guessed or omitted to give them further thought. Review other answers if you have time.

10) Return your test materials

If you are ready to leave before others have finished or time is called, take ALL your materials to the monitor and leave quietly. Never take any test material with you. The monitor can discover whose papers are not complete, and taking a test booklet may be grounds for disqualification.

VIII. EXAMINATION TECHNIQUES

1) Read the general instructions carefully. These are usually printed on the first page of the exam booklet. As a rule, these instructions refer to the timing of the examination; the fact that you should not start work until the signal and must stop work at a signal, etc. If there are any *special* instructions, such as a choice of questions to be answered, make sure that you note this instruction carefully.

2) When you are ready to start work on the examination, that is as soon as the signal has been given, read the instructions to each question booklet, underline any key words or phrases, such as *least, best, outline, describe* and the like. In this way you will tend to answer as requested rather than discover on reviewing your paper that you *listed without describing*, that you selected the *worst* choice rather than the *best* choice, etc.

3) If the examination is of the objective or multiple-choice type – that is, each question will also give a series of possible answers: A, B, C or D, and you are called upon to select the best answer and write the letter next to that answer on your answer paper – it is advisable to start answering each question in turn. There may be anywhere from 50 to 100 such questions in the three or four hours allotted and you can see how much time would be taken if you read through all the questions before beginning to answer any. Furthermore, if you come across a question or group of questions which you know would be difficult to answer, it would undoubtedly affect your handling of all the other questions.

4) If the examination is of the essay type and contains but a few questions, it is a moot point as to whether you should read all the questions before starting to answer any one. Of course, if you are given a choice – say five out of seven and the like – then it is essential to read all the questions so you can eliminate the two that are most difficult. If, however, you are asked to answer all the questions, there may be danger in trying to answer the easiest one first because you may find that you will spend too much time on it. The best technique is to answer the first question, then proceed to the second, etc.

5) Time your answers. Before the exam begins, write down the time it started, then add the time allowed for the examination and write down the time it must be completed, then divide the time available somewhat as follows:

- If 3-1/2 hours are allowed, that would be 210 minutes. If you have 80 objective-type questions, that would be an average of 2-1/2 minutes per question. Allow yourself no more than 2 minutes per question, or a total of 160 minutes, which will permit about 50 minutes to review.
- If for the time allotment of 210 minutes there are 7 essay questions to answer, that would average about 30 minutes a question. Give yourself only 25 minutes per question so that you have about 35 minutes to review.

6) The most important instruction is to *read each question* and make sure you know what is wanted. The second most important instruction is to *time yourself properly* so that you answer every question. The third most important instruction is to *answer every question*. Guess if you have to but include something for each question. Remember that you will receive no credit for a blank and will probably receive some credit if you write something in answer to an essay question. If you guess a letter – say "B" for a multiple-choice question – you may have guessed right. If you leave a blank as an answer to a multiple-choice question, the examiners may respect your feelings but it will not add a point to your score. Some exams may penalize you for wrong answers, so in such cases *only*, you may not want to guess unless you have some basis for your answer.

7) Suggestions
   a. Objective-type questions
      1. Examine the question booklet for proper sequence of pages and questions
      2. Read all instructions carefully
      3. Skip any question which seems too difficult; return to it after all other questions have been answered
      4. Apportion your time properly; do not spend too much time on any single question or group of questions
      5. Note and underline key words – *all, most, fewest, least, best, worst, same, opposite,* etc.
      6. Pay particular attention to negatives
      7. Note unusual option, e.g., unduly long, short, complex, different or similar in content to the body of the question
      8. Observe the use of "hedging" words – *probably, may, most likely,* etc.
      9. Make sure that your answer is put next to the same number as the question
      10. Do not second-guess unless you have good reason to believe the second answer is definitely more correct
      11. Cross out original answer if you decide another answer is more accurate; do not erase until you are ready to hand your paper in
      12. Answer all questions; guess unless instructed otherwise
      13. Leave time for review

   b. Essay questions
      1. Read each question carefully
      2. Determine exactly what is wanted. Underline key words or phrases.
      3. Decide on outline or paragraph answer

4. Include many different points and elements unless asked to develop any one or two points or elements
5. Show impartiality by giving pros and cons unless directed to select one side only
6. Make and write down any assumptions you find necessary to answer the questions
7. Watch your English, grammar, punctuation and choice of words
8. Time your answers; don't crowd material

8) Answering the essay question

Most essay questions can be answered by framing the specific response around several key words or ideas. Here are a few such key words or ideas:

M's: manpower, materials, methods, money, management
P's: purpose, program, policy, plan, procedure, practice, problems, pitfalls, personnel, public relations

a. Six basic steps in handling problems:
1. Preliminary plan and background development
2. Collect information, data and facts
3. Analyze and interpret information, data and facts
4. Analyze and develop solutions as well as make recommendations
5. Prepare report and sell recommendations
6. Install recommendations and follow up effectiveness

b. Pitfalls to avoid
1. *Taking things for granted* – A statement of the situation does not necessarily imply that each of the elements is necessarily true; for example, a complaint may be invalid and biased so that all that can be taken for granted is that a complaint has been registered
2. *Considering only one side of a situation* – Wherever possible, indicate several alternatives and then point out the reasons you selected the best one
3. *Failing to indicate follow up* – Whenever your answer indicates action on your part, make certain that you will take proper follow-up action to see how successful your recommendations, procedures or actions turn out to be
4. *Taking too long in answering any single question* – Remember to time your answers properly

IX. AFTER THE TEST

Scoring procedures differ in detail among civil service jurisdictions although the general principles are the same. Whether the papers are hand-scored or graded by machine we have described, they are nearly always graded by number. That is, the person who marks the paper knows only the number – never the name – of the applicant. Not until all the papers have been graded will they be matched with names. If other tests, such as training and experience or oral interview ratings have been given, scores will be combined. Different parts of the examination usually have different weights. For example, the written test might count 60 percent of the final grade, and a rating of training and experience 40 percent. In many jurisdictions, veterans will have a certain number of points added to their grades.

After the final grade has been determined, the names are placed in grade order and an eligible list is established. There are various methods for resolving ties between those who get the same final grade – probably the most common is to place first the name of the person whose application was received first. Job offers are made from the eligible list in the order the names appear on it. You will be notified of your grade and your rank as soon as all these computations have been made. This will be done as rapidly as possible.

People who are found to meet the requirements in the announcement are called "eligibles." Their names are put on a list of eligible candidates. An eligible's chances of getting a job depend on how high he stands on this list and how fast agencies are filling jobs from the list.

When a job is to be filled from a list of eligibles, the agency asks for the names of people on the list of eligibles for that job. When the civil service commission receives this request, it sends to the agency the names of the three people highest on this list. Or, if the job to be filled has specialized requirements, the office sends the agency the names of the top three persons who meet these requirements from the general list.

The appointing officer makes a choice from among the three people whose names were sent to him. If the selected person accepts the appointment, the names of the others are put back on the list to be considered for future openings.

That is the rule in hiring from all kinds of eligible lists, whether they are for typist, carpenter, chemist, or something else. For every vacancy, the appointing officer has his choice of any one of the top three eligibles on the list. This explains why the person whose name is on top of the list sometimes does not get an appointment when some of the persons lower on the list do. If the appointing officer chooses the second or third eligible, the No. 1 eligible does not get a job at once, but stays on the list until he is appointed or the list is terminated.

X. HOW TO PASS THE INTERVIEW TEST

The examination for which you applied requires an oral interview test. You have already taken the written test and you are now being called for the interview test – the final part of the formal examination.

You may think that it is not possible to prepare for an interview test and that there are no procedures to follow during an interview. Our purpose is to point out some things you can do in advance that will help you and some good rules to follow and pitfalls to avoid while you are being interviewed.

What is an interview supposed to test?
The written examination is designed to test the technical knowledge and competence of the candidate; the oral is designed to evaluate intangible qualities, not readily measured otherwise, and to establish a list showing the relative fitness of each candidate – as measured against his competitors – for the position sought. Scoring is not on the basis of "right" and "wrong," but on a sliding scale of values ranging from "not passable" to "outstanding." As a matter of fact, it is possible to achieve a relatively low score without a single "incorrect" answer because of evident weakness in the qualities being measured.

Occasionally, an examination may consist entirely of an oral test – either an individual or a group oral. In such cases, information is sought concerning the technical knowledges and abilities of the candidate, since there has been no written examination for this purpose. More commonly, however, an oral test is used to supplement a written examination.

Who conducts interviews?

The composition of oral boards varies among different jurisdictions. In nearly all, a representative of the personnel department serves as chairman. One of the members of the board may be a representative of the department in which the candidate would work. In some cases, "outside experts" are used, and, frequently, a businessman or some other representative of the general public is asked to serve. Labor and management or other special groups may be represented. The aim is to secure the services of experts in the appropriate field.

However the board is composed, it is a good idea (and not at all improper or unethical) to ascertain in advance of the interview who the members are and what groups they represent. When you are introduced to them, you will have some idea of their backgrounds and interests, and at least you will not stutter and stammer over their names.

What should be done before the interview?

While knowledge about the board members is useful and takes some of the surprise element out of the interview, there is other preparation which is more substantive. It *is* possible to prepare for an oral interview – in several ways:

1) Keep a copy of your application and review it carefully before the interview

This may be the only document before the oral board, and the starting point of the interview. Know what education and experience you have listed there, and the sequence and dates of all of it. Sometimes the board will ask you to review the highlights of your experience for them; you should not have to hem and haw doing it.

2) Study the class specification and the examination announcement

Usually, the oral board has one or both of these to guide them. The qualities, characteristics or knowledges required by the position sought are stated in these documents. They offer valuable clues as to the nature of the oral interview. For example, if the job involves supervisory responsibilities, the announcement will usually indicate that knowledge of modern supervisory methods and the qualifications of the candidate as a supervisor will be tested. If so, you can expect such questions, frequently in the form of a hypothetical situation which you are expected to solve. NEVER go into an oral without knowledge of the duties and responsibilities of the job you seek.

3) Think through each qualification required

Try to visualize the kind of questions you would ask if you were a board member. How well could you answer them? Try especially to appraise your own knowledge and background in each area, *measured against the job sought*, and identify any areas in which you are weak. Be critical and realistic – do not flatter yourself.

4) Do some general reading in areas in which you feel you may be weak

For example, if the job involves supervision and your past experience has NOT, some general reading in supervisory methods and practices, particularly in the field of human relations, might be useful. Do NOT study agency procedures or detailed manuals. The oral board will be testing your understanding and capacity, not your memory.

5) Get a good night's sleep and watch your general health and mental attitude

You will want a clear head at the interview. Take care of a cold or any other minor ailment, and of course, no hangovers.

What should be done on the day of the interview?

Now comes the day of the interview itself. Give yourself plenty of time to get there. Plan to arrive somewhat ahead of the scheduled time, particularly if your appointment is in the fore part of the day. If a previous candidate fails to appear, the board might be ready for you a bit early. By early afternoon an oral board is almost invariably behind schedule if there are many candidates, and you may have to wait. Take along a book or magazine to read, or your application to review, but leave any extraneous material in the waiting room when you go in for your interview. In any event, relax and compose yourself.

The matter of dress is important. The board is forming impressions about you – from your experience, your manners, your attitude, and your appearance. Give your personal appearance careful attention. Dress your best, but not your flashiest. Choose conservative, appropriate clothing, and be sure it is immaculate. This is a business interview, and your appearance should indicate that you regard it as such. Besides, being well groomed and properly dressed will help boost your confidence.

Sooner or later, someone will call your name and escort you into the interview room. *This is it.* From here on you are on your own. It is too late for any more preparation. But remember, you asked for this opportunity to prove your fitness, and you are here because your request was granted.

What happens when you go in?

The usual sequence of events will be as follows: The clerk (who is often the board stenographer) will introduce you to the chairman of the oral board, who will introduce you to the other members of the board. Acknowledge the introductions before you sit down. Do not be surprised if you find a microphone facing you or a stenotypist sitting by. Oral interviews are usually recorded in the event of an appeal or other review.

Usually the chairman of the board will open the interview by reviewing the highlights of your education and work experience from your application – primarily for the benefit of the other members of the board, as well as to get the material into the record. Do not interrupt or comment unless there is an error or significant misinterpretation; if that is the case, do not hesitate. But do not quibble about insignificant matters. Also, he will usually ask you some question about your education, experience or your present job – partly to get you to start talking and to establish the interviewing "rapport." He may start the actual questioning, or turn it over to one of the other members. Frequently, each member undertakes the questioning on a particular area, one in which he is perhaps most competent, so you can expect each member to participate in the examination. Because time is limited, you may also expect some rather abrupt switches in the direction the questioning takes, so do not be upset by it. Normally, a board member will not pursue a single line of questioning unless he discovers a particular strength or weakness.

After each member has participated, the chairman will usually ask whether any member has any further questions, then will ask you if you have anything you wish to add. Unless you are expecting this question, it may floor you. Worse, it may start you off on an extended, extemporaneous speech. The board is not usually seeking more information. The question is principally to offer you a last opportunity to present further qualifications or to indicate that you have nothing to add. So, if you feel that a significant qualification or characteristic has been overlooked, it is proper to point it out in a sentence or so. Do not compliment the board on the thoroughness of their examination – they have been sketchy, and you know it. If you wish, merely say, "No thank you, I have nothing further to add." This is a point where you can "talk yourself out" of a good impression or fail to present an important bit of information. Remember, *you close the interview yourself.*

The chairman will then say, "That is all, Mr. ______, thank you." Do not be startled; the interview is over, and quicker than you think. Thank him, gather your belongings and take your leave. Save your sigh of relief for the other side of the door.

How to put your best foot forward

Throughout this entire process, you may feel that the board individually and collectively is trying to pierce your defenses, seek out your hidden weaknesses and embarrass and confuse you. Actually, this is not true. They are obliged to make an appraisal of your qualifications for the job you are seeking, and they want to see you in your best light. Remember, they must interview all candidates and a non-cooperative candidate may become a failure in spite of their best efforts to bring out his qualifications. Here are 15 suggestions that will help you:

1) Be natural – Keep your attitude confident, not cocky

If you are not confident that you can do the job, do not expect the board to be. Do not apologize for your weaknesses, try to bring out your strong points. The board is interested in a positive, not negative, presentation. Cockiness will antagonize any board member and make him wonder if you are covering up a weakness by a false show of strength.

2) Get comfortable, but don't lounge or sprawl

Sit erectly but not stiffly. A careless posture may lead the board to conclude that you are careless in other things, or at least that you are not impressed by the importance of the occasion. Either conclusion is natural, even if incorrect. Do not fuss with your clothing, a pencil or an ashtray. Your hands may occasionally be useful to emphasize a point; do not let them become a point of distraction.

3) Do not wisecrack or make small talk

This is a serious situation, and your attitude should show that you consider it as such. Further, the time of the board is limited – they do not want to waste it, and neither should you.

4) Do not exaggerate your experience or abilities

In the first place, from information in the application or other interviews and sources, the board may know more about you than you think. Secondly, you probably will not get away with it. An experienced board is rather adept at spotting such a situation, so do not take the chance.

5) If you know a board member, do not make a point of it, yet do not hide it

Certainly you are not fooling him, and probably not the other members of the board. Do not try to take advantage of your acquaintanceship – it will probably do you little good.

6) Do not dominate the interview

Let the board do that. They will give you the clues – do not assume that you have to do all the talking. Realize that the board has a number of questions to ask you, and do not try to take up all the interview time by showing off your extensive knowledge of the answer to the first one.

7) Be attentive

You only have 20 minutes or so, and you should keep your attention at its sharpest throughout. When a member is addressing a problem or question to you, give him your undivided attention. Address your reply principally to him, but do not exclude the other board members.

8) Do not interrupt

A board member may be stating a problem for you to analyze. He will ask you a question when the time comes. Let him state the problem, and wait for the question.

9) Make sure you understand the question

Do not try to answer until you are sure what the question is. If it is not clear, restate it in your own words or ask the board member to clarify it for you. However, do not haggle about minor elements.

10) Reply promptly but not hastily

A common entry on oral board rating sheets is "candidate responded readily," or "candidate hesitated in replies." Respond as promptly and quickly as you can, but do not jump to a hasty, ill-considered answer.

11) Do not be peremptory in your answers

A brief answer is proper – but do not fire your answer back. That is a losing game from your point of view. The board member can probably ask questions much faster than you can answer them.

12) Do not try to create the answer you think the board member wants

He is interested in what kind of mind you have and how it works – not in playing games. Furthermore, he can usually spot this practice and will actually grade you down on it.

13) Do not switch sides in your reply merely to agree with a board member

Frequently, a member will take a contrary position merely to draw you out and to see if you are willing and able to defend your point of view. Do not start a debate, yet do not surrender a good position. If a position is worth taking, it is worth defending.

14) Do not be afraid to admit an error in judgment if you are shown to be wrong

The board knows that you are forced to reply without any opportunity for careful consideration. Your answer may be demonstrably wrong. If so, admit it and get on with the interview.

15) Do not dwell at length on your present job

The opening question may relate to your present assignment. Answer the question but do not go into an extended discussion. You are being examined for a *new* job, not your present one. As a matter of fact, try to phrase ALL your answers in terms of the job for which you are being examined.

Basis of Rating

Probably you will forget most of these "do's" and "don'ts" when you walk into the oral interview room. Even remembering them all will not ensure you a passing grade. Perhaps you did not have the qualifications in the first place. But remembering them will help you to put your best foot forward, without treading on the toes of the board members.

Rumor and popular opinion to the contrary notwithstanding, an oral board wants you to make the best appearance possible. They know you are under pressure – but they also want to see how you respond to it as a guide to what your reaction would be under the pressures of the job you seek. They will be influenced by the degree of poise you display, the personal traits you show and the manner in which you respond.

ABOUT THIS BOOK

This book contains tests divided into Examination Sections. Go through each test, answering every question in the margin. At the end of each test look at the answer key and check your answers. On the ones you got wrong, look at the right answer choice and learn. Do not fill in the answers first. Do not memorize the questions and answers, but understand the answer and principles involved. On your test, the questions will likely be different from the samples. Questions are changed and new ones added. If you understand these past questions you should have success with any changes that arise. Tests may consist of several types of questions. We have additional books on each subject should more study be advisable or necessary for you. Finally, the more you study, the better prepared you will be. This book is intended to be the last thing you study before you walk into the examination room. Prior study of relevant texts is also recommended. NLC publishes some of these in our Fundamental Series. Knowledge and good sense are important factors in passing your exam. Good luck also helps. So now study this Passbook, absorb the material contained within and take that knowledge into the examination. Then do your best to pass that exam.

EXAMINATION SECTION

EXAMINATION SECTION
TEST 1

DIRECTIONS: Each question or incomplete statement is followed by several suggested answers or completions. Select the one that BEST answers the question or completes the statement. *PRINT THE LETTER OF THE CORRECT ANSWER IN THE SPACE AT THE RIGHT.*

Questions 1-10.

DIRECTIONS: For each of the sentences given below, numbered 1 through 10, select from the following choices the MOST correct choice and print your choice in the space at the right. Select as your answer:
- A – if the statement contains an unnecessary word of expression
- B – if the statement contains a slang term or expression ordinarily not acceptable in government report writing
- C – if the statement contains an old-fashioned word or expression, where a concrete, plain term would be more useful
- D – if the statement contains no major faults

1.   Every one of us should try harder.   1.____

2.   Yours of the first instant has been received.   2.____

3.   We will have to do a real snow job on him.   3.____

4.   I shall contact him next Thursday.   4.____

5.   None of us were invited to the meeting with the community.   5.____

6.   We got this here job to do.   6.____

7.   She could not help but see the mistake in the checkbook.   7.____

8.   Don't bug the Director about the report.   8.____

9.   I beg to inform you that your letter has been received.   9.____

10.   This project is all screwed up.   10.____

Questions 11-15.

DIRECTIONS: Read the following Inter-office Memo. Then answer Questions 11 through 15 based ONLY on the memo.

INTER-OFFICE MEMORANDUM

To: *Alma Robinson, Human Resources Aide*
From: *Frank Shields, Social Worker*

I would like to have you help Mr. Edward Tunney who is trying to raise his two children by himself. He needs to learn to improve the physical care of his children and especially of his daughter Helen, age 9. She is avoided and ridiculed at school because her hair is uncombed, her teeth not properly cleaned, her clothing torn, wrinkled and dirty, as well as shabby and poorly fitted. The teachers and school officials have contacted the Department and the social worker for two years about Helen. She is not able to make friends because of these problems. I have talked to Mr. Tunney about improvements for the child's clothing, hair, and hygiene. He tends to deny these things are problems, but is cooperative, and a second person showing him the importance of better physical care for Helen would be helpful.

Perhaps you could teach Helen how to fix her own hair. She has all the materials. I would also like you to form your own opinion of the sanitary conditions in the home and how they could be improved.

Mr. Tunney is expecting your visit and is willing to talk with you about ways he can help with these problems.

11. In the above memorandum, the Human Resources Aide is being asked to help Mr. Tunney to   11.____

    A. improve the learning habits of his children
    B. enable his children to make friends at school
    C. take responsibility for the upbringing of his children
    D. give attention to the grooming and cleanliness of his children

12. This case was brought to the attention of the social worker by   12.____

    A. government officials
    B. teachers and school officials
    C. the Department
    D. Mr. Tunney

13. In general, Mr. Tunney's attitude with regard to his children could BEST be described as   13.____

    A. interested in correcting the obvious problems, but unable to do so alone
    B. unwilling to follow the advice of those who are trying to help
    C. concerned, but unaware of the seriousness of these problems
    D. interested in helping them, but afraid of taking the advice of the social worker

14. Which of the following actions has NOT been suggested as a possible step for the Human Resources Aide to take?   14.____

    A. Help Helen to learn to care for herself by teaching her grooming skills
    B. Determine ways of improvement through information gathered on a home visit
    C. Discuss her own views on Helen's problems with school officials
    D. Ask Mr. Tunney in what ways he believes the physical care may be improved

15. According to the memo, the Human Resources Aide is ESPECIALLY being asked to observe and form her own opinions about   15.____

    A. the relationship between Mr. Tunney and the school officials
    B. Helen's attitude toward her classmates and teacher
    C. the sanitary conditions in the home
    D. the reasons Mr. Tunney is not cooperative with the agency

16. In one day, an aide receives 18 inquiries by phone and 27 inquiries in person. What percentage of the inquiries received that day were by phone?   16.____

    A. 33%   B. 40%   C. 45%   D. 60%

17. If the weekly pay checks for 5 part-time employees are: $129.32, $162.74, $143.67, $135.75, and $156.56, then the combined weekly income for the 5 employees is   17.____

    A. $727.84   B. $728.04   C. $730.84   D. $737.04

18. Suppose that there are 17 aides working in an office where many community complaints are received by telephone. In one ten-day period, 4250 calls were received. If the same number of calls were received each day, and the aides divided the work load equally, about how many calls did each aide respond to daily?   18.____

    A. 25   B. 35   C. 75   D. 250

19. Suppose that an assignment was divided among 5 aides. If the first aide spent 67 hours on the assignment, the second aide spent 95 hours, the third aide spent 52 hours, the fourth aide spent 78 hours, and the fifth aide spent 103 hours, what was the AVERAGE amount of time spent by each aide on the assignment?
_______ hours.   19.____

    A. 71   B. 75   C. 79   D. 83

20. If there are 240 employees in a center and 1/3 are absent on the day of a bad snow-storm, how many employees were at work in the center on that day?   20.____

    A. 80   B. 120   C. 160   D. 200

KEY (CORRECT ANSWERS)

1.	D	11.	D
2.	C	12.	B
3.	B	13.	C
4.	D	14.	C
5.	D	15.	C
6.	B	16.	B
7.	D	17.	B
8.	B	18.	A
9.	C	19.	C
10.	B	20.	C

TEST 2

DIRECTIONS: Each question or incomplete statement is followed by several suggested answers or completions. Select the one that BEST answers the question or completes the statement. *PRINT THE LETTER OF THE CORRECT ANSWER IN THE SPACE AT THE RIGHT.*

1. Suppose that an aide takes 25 minutes to prepare a letter to a client. If the aide is assigned to prepare 9 letters on a certain day, how much time should she set aside for this task? ______ hours. 1.____

   A. 3 3/4   B. 4 1/4   C. 4 3/4   D. 5 1/4

2. Suppose that a certain center uses both Form A and Form B in the course of its daily work, and that Form A is used 4 times as often as Form B. If the total number of both forms used in one week is 750, how many times was Form A used? 2.____

   A. 100   B. 200   C. 400   D. 600

3. Suppose a center has a budget of $1092.70 from which 8 desks costing $78.05 apiece must be bought? How many ADDITIONAL desks can be ordered from this budget after the 8 desks have been purchased? 3.____

   A. 4   B. 6   C. 9   D. 14

4. When researching a particular case, a team of 16 aides was asked to check through 234 folders to obtain the necessary information. If half the aides worked twice as fast as the other half, and the slow group checked through 12 folders each hour, about how long would it take to complete the assignment? ______ hours. 4.____

   A. $4\frac{1}{4}$ B. 5   C. 6   D. $6\frac{1}{2}$

5. The difference in the cost of two printers is $28.32. If the less expensive printer costs $153.61, what is the cost of the other printer? 5.____

   A. $171.93   B. $172.03   C. $181.93   D. $182.03

Questions 6-8.

DIRECTIONS: Questions 6 through 8 are to be answered on the basis of the following information contained on a sample page of a payroll book.

Emp. No.	Name of Employee	M	T	W	Th	F	Total Hours Worked	Pay PerHour	Total Wages
1	James Smith	8	8	8	8	8			$480.00
2	Gloria Jones	8	7 3/4	7		7 1/2		$16.00	$560.00
3	Robert Adams	6	6	71/2	71/2	8 3/4		$18.28	

6. The pay per hour of Employee No. 1 is

    A. $12.00   B. $13.72   C. $15.00   D. $19.20

6.____

7. The number of hours that Employee No. 2 worked on Friday is

    A. 4   B. 5 1/2   C. 4.63   D. 4 3/4

7.____

8. The total wages for Employee No. 3 is

    A. $636.92   B. $648.94   C. $661.04   D. $672.96

8.____

9. As a rule, the FIRST step in writing a check should be to

    A. number the check
    B. write in the payee's name
    C. tear out the check stub
    D. write the purpose of the check in the space provided at the bottom

9.____

10. If an error is made when writing a check, the MOST widely accepted procedure is to

    A. draw a line through the error and initial it
    B. destroy both the check and check stub by tearing into small pieces
    C. erase the error if it does not occur in the amount of the check
    D. write *Void* across both the check and check stub and save them

10.____

11. The check that is MOST easily cashed is one that is

    A. not signed   B. made payable to *Cash*
    C. post-dated   D. endorsed in part

11.____

12.

12.____

No. 103	$ 142. 77
May 14	
To Alan Jacobs	
For Wages (5/6-5/10)	

Bal. Bro't For ' d	2340. 63
Amt. Deposited	205. 24
Total	
Amt. This Check	142. 77
Bal. Car'd For ' d	

The balance to be carried forward on the check stub above is
    A. $2,278.16   B. $1,992.62   C. $2,688.64   D. $2,403.10

13. The procedure for reconciling a bank statement consists of ______ the bank balance and ______ the checkbook balance.

    A. *adding* outstanding checks to; *subtracting* the service and check charges from
    B. *subtracting* the service charge from; *subtracting* outstanding checks from
    C. *subtracting* the service charge from; *adding* outstanding checks to
    D. *subtracting* outstanding checks from; *subtracting* the service and check charges from

13.____

14. An employee makes $15.70 an hour and receives time-and-a-half in overtime pay for every hour more than 40 in a given week. If the employee works 47 hours, the employee's total wages for that week would be   14._____

    A. $792.85   B. $837.90   C. $875.25   D. $1,106.85

15. A high-speed copier can make 25,000 copies before periodic service is required. Before this service is necessary, _____ copies of a 137-page document can be printed.   15._____

    A. 211   B. 204   C. 190   D. 178

16. An aide is typing a letter to the James Weldon Johnson Head Start Center. To be sure that a Mr. Joseph Maxwell reads it, an attention line is typed below the inside address. The salutation should, therefore, read: 16._____

    A. To Whom It May Concern: B. Dear Mr. Maxwell:
    C. Gentlemen: D. Dear Joseph:

17. When describing the advantages of the numeric filing system, it is NOT true that it   17._____

    A. is the most accurate of all methods
    B. allows for unlimited expansion according to the needs of the agency
    C. is a system useful for filing letters directly according to name or subject
    D. allows for cross-referencing

18. In writing a letter for your Center, the PURPOSE of the letter should usually be stated in   18._____

    A. the first paragraph. This assists the reader in making more sense of the letter.
    B. the second paragraph. The first paragraph should be used to confirm receipt of the letter being answered
    C. the last paragraph. The first paragraphs should be used to build up to the purpose of the letter.
    D. any paragraph. Each letter has a different purpose and the letter should conform to that purpose.

19. If you open a personal letter addressed to another aide by mistake, the one of the following actions which it would generally be BEST for you to take is to   19._____

    A. reseal the envelope or place the contents in another envelope and pass it on to the employee
    B. place the letter inside the envelope, indicate under your initials that it was opened in error and give it to the employee
    C. personally give the employee the letter without any explanation
    D. ignore your error, attach the envelope to the letter, and give it out in the usual manner

20. Of the following, the MAIN purpose of the head start program is to   20._____

    A. provide programs for pre-school development of children
    B. provide children between the ages of 6 and 12 with after-school activity
    C. establish a system for providing care for teenage youngsters with working parents
    D. supervise centers providing 24-hour child care

KEY (CORRECT ANSWERS)

1.	A		11.	B
2.	D		12.	D
3.	B		13.	D
4.	D		14.	A
5.	C		15.	D
6.	A		16.	C
7.	D		17.	C
8.	B		18.	A
9.	A		19.	B
10.	D		20.	A

———

EXAMINATION SECTION
TEST 1

DIRECTIONS: Each question or incomplete statement is followed by several suggested answers or completions. Select the one that BEST answers the question or completes the statement. *PRINT THE LETTER OF THE CORRECT ANSWER IN THE SPACE AT THE RIGHT.*

1. Which of the following statements is TRUE?   1.____

    A. The goal of normalization is to allow one to do whatever one likes.
    B. Normalization involves making a person become normal.
    C. Normalization advocates that whenever possible, people's perceptions of developmentally disabled individuals must be enhanced or improved.
    D. Normalization advocates encouraging the developmentally disabled to be just like everyone else.

2. It is important to view the developmentally disabled as   2.____

    A. helpless
    B. unable to make decisions
    C. deviant
    D. none of the above

3. All of the following would be considered good practice EXCEPT   3.____

    A. providing residential services in the community, rather than in an isolated area
    B. placing residential homes next to rural prisons
    C. providing access in residences to accommodate those who are non-ambulatory
    D. avoiding excessive rules that tend to separate staff from residents

4. All of the following are true in normalization EXCEPT   4.____

    A. family involvement in normalization is usually not helpful to achieving the goal
    B. clients should be involved, when possible, in selecting programming in order to develop independence
    C. program options should emphasize autonomy, independence, integration, and productivity
    D. it is a good idea when possible to have day programming located apart from the living setting

5. Benefits of normalization include all of the following EXCEPT   5.____

    A. development of self-confidence and self-esteem in the developmentally disabled
    B. social integration of the developmentally disabled
    C. positive changes in societal attitudes regarding the developmentally disabled
    D. societal acceptance of deviance

6. All of the following statements are true EXCEPT: 6.____

    A. Normalization means that normal conditions of life should be made available to developmentally disabled people
    B. Attitudes toward the mentally retarded have a great effect on the way they are treated, and, consequently, on their chances for living a productive, normal life

"

C. It is highly unlikely that efforts at normalization will succeed in most communities
D. What is normal or typical in one society may not be normal or typical in another

7. In normalization, the means used to teach a skill are as important as the skill itself. In teaching adults, which of the following would be MOST appropriate?   7.____

   A. Working individually with someone after dinner in order to teach him or her how to brush their teeth
   B. Teaching pouring skills with sand in a sandbox
   C. Teaching how to button clothes by using a doll for practice
   D. Teaching how to tie shoelaces by first working With a baby shoe

8. Which of the following statements is TRUE?   8.____

   A. Residents' chore duties in a community residence should only change three times a year.
   B. Entrance into a community residence should be solely determined by an individual's need for a place to live.
   C. Using a task analysis for a client would involve breaking down a complex task into smaller, more understandable parts.
   D. Clients should be allowed to eat when and what they choose.

9. Select the one statement below that is NOT true of supervised community residences. A supervised community residence   9.____

   A. can provide short-term residence for individuals who need only training and experience in activities of daily living after a period of institutionalization or as an alternative to institutionalization
   B. can provide an institutional setting for those people who need it
   C. can provide long-term residence for individuals who are unlikely to acquire the skills necessary for more independent living
   D. usually requires staff on site at all times

10. All of the following are goals of community residences EXCEPT   10.____

   A. providing a home environment for developmentally disabled persons
   B. providing a setting where clients can learn the skills necessary to live in the least restrictive environment
   C. providing a setting where the developmentally disabled can acquire the skills necessary to live as independently as possible
   D. the community residence allows for the maximum level of independence inconsistent with a person's disability and functional level

11. All of the following statements are true EXCEPT: 11.____

   A. A community residence does not need to adhere to the principle of normalization in its physical or social structure
   B. The term least restrictive environment refers to an environment which most resembles that of non-handicapped peers where the needs of developmentally disabled persons can be met

C. A person's length of stay in a community residence extends only until a person has attained the skills and motivation to function successfully in a less restrictive setting
D. The purposes of a community residence may vary so that people with different ranges of abilities and levels of functioning may be served

12. All of the following statements are true EXCEPT: 12._____

    A. Developmentally disabled persons residing in community residences must be afforded privacy, personal space, and freedom of access to the house as is consistent with their age and program needs
    B. Transportation should be available from the nearest institution so that people in community residences have access to the community
    C. The service needs of each person in a community residence should be individually planned by an interdisciplinary team
    D. An interdisciplinary team should include staff of the community residence, providers of program and support services, and, if appropriate, the developmentally disabled person's correspondent

13. All of the following statements are true EXCEPT: 13._____

    A. Supportive community residences are not required to provide staff on site 24 hours a day
    B. Residents in supervised community residences may need more assistance in activities of daily living than persons residing in supportive community residences
    C. An aim of a community residence is to maintain a family and home-like environment
    D. Those living in a community residence shall spend at least three hours per weekday and one evening per week in programs and activities at the residence

14. In working in treatment teams, it is MOST important for team members to 14._____

    A. communicate effectively with each other
    B. keep morale high
    C. attend meetings on time
    D. enjoy working with each other

15. All of the following statements are true EXCEPT: 15._____

    A. In teaching self-care skills, many tasks may need to be divided into sub-parts
    B. Tasks which are easiest to learn should generally be taught first
    C. Changes in routine are very helpful when teaching the mentally retarded a new skill
    D. The severely retarded do not learn as well from verbal instruction as they do from demonstration of a skill

16. All of the following statements are true EXCEPT: 16._____

    A. It is important to evaluate the client's readiness to attempt learning a particular task before starting to teach the task
    B. It is better to do a task for a client if the task may take much time and effort on his or her part
    C. People generally learn faster when their efforts lead to an enjoyable activity
    D. It is best when teaching a certain skill to begin with a small group when possible

17. All of the following statements are true EXCEPT:

    A. The expectations of a staff person of how well a client will be able to perform a certain task can influence daily living skills
    B. Environmental factors can influence daily living skills
    C. After seeing a skill demonstrated, a client should practice the skill
    D. A client will make a greater effort if he or she feels ill at ease with the instructor, and knows the instructor will become impatient if he or she continues to make mistakes

17.____

18. Of the following, the BEST way to teach a client an activity of daily living is to

    A. describe the steps to the client
    B. read the directions to the client
    C. break the activity into steps and have the client learn one step at a time
    D. have a client who can perform the task teach the client who cannot

18.____

19. All of the following are important steps in teaching a living skill EXCEPT

    A. defining the skill clearly
    B. determining the size of the skill
    C. breaking down each major step into substeps and sub-substeps as necessary
    D. rewarding the accomplishment of each step with candy

19.____

20. When teaching a daily living skill, it is important to keep in mind all of the following EXCEPT

    A. using concrete and specific language
    B. punishment can be a highly effective learning device
    C. matching the size of the skill to the client's ability level
    D. demonstrating what you want the resident to do

20.____

KEY (CORRECT ANSWERS)

1.	C	11.	A
2.	D	12.	B
3.	B	13.	D
4.	A	14.	A
5.	D	15.	C
6.	C	16.	B
7.	A	17.	D
8.	C	18.	C
9.	B	19.	D
10.	D	20.	B

TEST 2

DIRECTIONS: Each question or incomplete statement is followed by several suggested answers or completions. Select the one that BEST answers the question or completes the statement. *PRINT THE LETTER OF THE CORRECT ANSWER IN THE SPACE AT THE RIGHT.*

1. All of the following would be considered qualities of a developmental disability EXCEPT the disability   1._____

    A.   may be attributable to mental retardation or autism
    B.   has continued or can be expected to continue indefinitely
    C.   can be easily overcome
    D.   may be attributable to cerebral palsy or neurological impairment

2. The condition of autism   2._____

    A.   applies to those people who have little or no control over their motor skills
    B.   is hereditary
    C.   is characterized by severe disorders of communication and behavior
    D.   begins most frequently in adulthood

3. Secondary childhood autism differs from primary childhood autism in that   3._____

    A.   primary childhood autism is more difficult to treat
    B.   secondary childhood autism is secondary to disturbances such as brain damage
    C.   secondary childhood autism is not as severe a disorder
    D.   secondary childhood autism is less likely to interfere with behavior patterns

4. Which of the following would be LEAST adversely affected by autism?   4._____

    A.   Interpersonal relations
    B.   Learning
    C.   Developmental rate and sequences
    D.   Motor skills

5. Which of the following statements is NOT true?   5._____

    A.   Cerebral palsy refers to a condition resulting from damage to the brain that may occur before, during or after birth and results in the loss of control over voluntary muscles in the body.
    B.   Ataxic cerebral palsy is characterized by an inability to maintain normal balance.
    C.   Someone with athetoid cerebral palsy would find it easier to maintain purposefulness of movements than someone with spastic cerebral palsy.
    D.   Mixed cerebral palsy refers to the combination of two or more of the following categories of cerebral palsy such as the spastic, athetoid, ataxic, tremor, and rigid types.

6. All of the following are true about epilepsy EXCEPT   6._____

    A.   epilepsy does not usually involve a loss of consciousness
    B.   an *aura* often appears to the individual before a *grand mal* seizure occurs

C. people experiencing *petit mal* seizures are seldom aware that a seizure has occurred
D. status epilepticus, psychomotor, and Jacksonian are all forms of epilepsy

7. All of the following statements are true of mental retardation EXCEPT: 7.____

  A. The prevalence of mental retardation in the general total population is less than 3% of the population
  B. Approximately 89% of the mentally retarded population is mildly retarded
  C. School-age children who are mildly retarded can usually acquire practical skills and useful reading and arithmetic skills
  D. Adults who are mildly retarded can not usually achieve social and vocational skills adequate for minimum self-support

8. Which of the following statements is NOT true of mental retardation?   8.____

  A. Approximately 6% of the mentally retarded population is moderately retarded (I.Q. 36-51), 3.5% of the mentally retarded population is severely retarded (I.Q. 20-35), and 1.5% of this population is profoundly retarded (I.Q. 19 and below).
  B. A profoundly retarded person could never achieve limited self-care.
  C. Moderately retarded adults may achieve self-maintenance in unskilled work or semi-skilled work under sheltered conditions.
  D. Severely retarded children can profit from systematic skills training.

9. All of the following refer to neurological impairment EXCEPT   9.____

  A. childhood aphasia is a condition characterized by the failure to develop, or difficulty in using, language and speech
  B. epilepsy
  C. minimal brain dysfunction is associated with deviations of the central nervous system
  D. neurological impairment refers to a group of disorders of the central nervous system characterized by dysfunction in one or more, but not all, skills affecting communicative, perceptual, cognitive, memory, attentional, motor control, and appropriate social behaviors

10. Which of the following statements is TRUE?   10.____

  A. Autistic children are below average in intelligence level.
  B. All cerebral palsied persons are mentally retarded.
  C. Once an epileptic seizure has started, it cannot be stopped.
  D. Autism is due to faulty early interactional patterns between child and mother.

11. All of the following are false EXCEPT   11.____

  A. recent investigations have found that parents of autistic children have no specific common personality traits and no unusual environmental stresses
  B. cerebral palsied persons cannot understand directions
  C. it is not true that unless controlled seizures can cause further brain damage
  D. the majority of the mentally retarded are in institutions

12. In serving the needs of autistic persons, the one of the following which is usually LEAST important is the need 12.____

    A. for training in social skills
    B. for language stimulation
    C. to deal with potentially self-injurious, repetitive, and aggressive behaviors
    D. to teach skills that would improve intelligence

13. In serving the needs of persons with cerebral palsy, the one of the following which is usually LEAST important is the need 13.____

    A. to experience normal movement and sensations as much as possible
    B. to develop fundamental movement patterns which the person can regulate
    C. for experience and guidance in social settings
    D. to restrict their environment

14. All of the following statements are true EXCEPT: 14.____

    A. It is important that epileptic persons have balanced diets
    B. Pica, a craving for unnatural food, occurs with all mentally retarded persons
    C. It has been projected that 50% of those individuals who have cerebral palsy are also mentally retarded
    D. When working with the mentally retarded, it is important to encourage sensory-motor stimulation, physical stimulation, language stimulation, social skills training, and the performance of daily living skills

15. When working with neurologically impaired persons, all of the following are true EXCEPT: 15.____

    A. There is usually a need for perceptual training
    B. It is important to keep in mind that an individual may know something one day and not know it the next
    C. It may be necessary to remove distracting stimuli
    D. It is important to keep in mind that neurologically impaired persons usually have substantially lower I.Q.'s than the average person

16. The developmentally disabled do NOT have the right to 16.____

    A. register and vote in elections
    B. marry
    C. confidentiality of records
    D. hit someone who teases them

17. Which of the following statements is TRUE? 17.____

    A. It is important for staff members not to make all of the choices for their mentally retarded clients.
    B. Distraction is not a good technique to use when trying to channel potentially violent or destructive behavior to a socially acceptable outlet.
    C. Severely and profoundly retarded children do not appear to have a strong need for personal contact.
    D. It is primarily the mildly or moderately retarded child that exhibits the behavior usually associated with mental retardation.

18. All of the following are causes of mental retardation EXCEPT   18.____

    A. organic defects
    B. brain lesions
    C. increased sexual activity
    D. chromosomal abnormalities

19. A mentally retarded patient who is *acting out*   19.____

    A. may be trying to communicate that he or she is physically uncomfortable or needs something
    B. should be ignored
    C. should be severely punished
    D. feels comfortable in his or her surroundings

20. In working with the developmentally disabled, all of the following would be appropriate EXCEPT   20.____

    A. remembering that seemingly small things, both positive and negative, can be very important to the client
    B. allowing choices whenever possible
    C. maintaining a calm, level-headed attitude during an anxiety-producing situation will reassure clients and help them relax and feel safer
    D. after basic self-help skills have been mastered, it is not necessary to encourage further development

---

KEY (CORRECT ANSWERS)

1.	C		11.	A
2.	C		12.	D
3.	B		13.	D
4.	D		14.	B
5.	C		15.	D
6.	A		16.	D
7.	D		17.	A
8.	B		18.	C
9.	B		19.	A
10.	C		20.	D

EXAMINATION SECTION
TEST 1

DIRECTIONS: Each question or incomplete statement is followed by several suggested answers or completions. Select the one that BEST answers the question or completes the statement. *PRINT THE LETTER OF THE CORRECT ANSWER IN THE SPACE AT THE RIGHT.*

1. Clinical observations and research on motor functioning of the intellectually disabled indicate 1.____

    A. there is a marked discrepancy in motor functioning between tasks requiring precise and those requiring complex movements
    B. there is a high degree of correspondence between general mental ability and motor performance
    C. there is no difference in the motor performance of moderately disabled and mildly disabled individuals
    D. degree of stimulation has no effect on motor performance

2. The incidence of the diagnosis of intellectual disability in males as compared with that of females is 2.____

    A. considerably higher   B. considerably lower
    C. slightly lower   D. about the same

3. In terms of their behavior and the causes of their disability, intellectually disabled children would be classified as a ______ group. 3.____

    A. very homogeneous   B. moderately homogeneous
    C. very heterogeneous   D. moderately heterogeneous

4. In terms of socioeconomic status, MOST disabled children come from families that in socioeconomic status 4.____

    A. are rated low
    B. range from middle class to high
    C. are middle class
    D. range the spectrum

5. While phenylketonuria accounts for a small fraction of intellectual disabilities, it is one of the few forms that can be 5.____

    A. identified as a causative agent in the first three months of pregnancy
    B. vitiated by early psychiatric treatment
    C. alleviated through strict adherence to a high phenyla-lanine diet
    D. prevented by specific medical intervention

6. A child who has been diagnosed as having cerebral aphasia shows ______ speech. 6.____

    A. lack of   B. perseverative   C. echolalic   D. repetitive

7. Follow-up studies indicate that the intellectually disabled tend to 7.____

    A. remain on their initial job because they are fearful of change
    B. change jobs frequently in their early post-school years
    C. move up the ladder of success as do non-disabled, but at a slower pace
    D. stabilize in one job or one area of work in their early post-school years

8. The PRIMARY objective of special education for the preponderance of the intellectually disabled is   8.____

    A. contribution to the community
    B. participation in family life
    C. adjustment to the neighborhood environment
    D. adjustment in a sheltered work situation

9. Disability resulting from organic impairment or birth injury has been classified as   9.____

    A. endogenous   B. familial
    C. primary amentia   D. exogenous

10. Resources in the community for treating the emotional problems of intellectually disabled children are   10.____

    A. more difficult to obtain than for non-disabled children
    B. under-utilized because of parental resistance to accepting disabilities
    C. under-utilized because the disabilities tend to mask emotional difficulties
    D. not effective with most types of disabled children

11. The disabled child who refuses to attend school and cries, throws up, and clings to the parent when it comes time to leave each morning is MOST probably showing symptoms of   11.____

    A. overdependence   B. school phobia
    C. psychopathic behavior   D. improper nutrition

12. One of the MOST promising developments in institutional care for the intellectually disabled was the   12.____

    A. addition of attendants to the inter-disciplinary staffs of installations
    B. organization of a well-rounded recreation program
    C. inclusion of psychotherapy in the institutional program
    D. establishment of a self-government program

13. The Arc is a(n)   13.____

    A. youth group for the disabled, similar in design to the 4-H Clubs
    B. group of non-professionals associated with the American Association on Mental Deficiency
    C. service and support organization for disabled individuals and their families
    D. association of teachers of the disabled, organized by the National Education Association

14. In MOST instances, parental inability to accept disabilities in their child as a fact can be attributed primarily to their   14.____

    A. feelings of guilt
    B. fear of being viewed as subnormal themselves
    C. lack of knowledge of children's development
    D. being too close to the child to see him objectively

15. Which one of the following descriptions MOST accurately characterizes the degree to which the intellectually disabled will be able to function in social-vocational areas when they reach adulthood?

    A. Little more than self-care
    B. Partial self-support in a supervised environment, such as a sheltered workshop
    C. Employment, when given assistance from medical personnel in correcting physical or emotional deficiencies
    D. Employment in the community with the aid of appropriate school and community agencies when necessary

15.____

16. The process whereby an individual acquires his moral, social, and emotional attitudes from the people with whom he comes in frequent contact is called

    A. projection
    B. introjection
    C. transfer of learning
    D. transference

16.____

17. A resident of working age, who has a permanent disability that is an employment handicap, is eligible for vocational rehabilitation if he

    A. is unemployable
    B. requires custodial care for an extended period of time
    C. is employable in a sheltered workshop only
    D. can become employable within a reasonable length of time

17.____

18. Of those listed below, the MOST likely jobs for the intellectually disabled are:

    A. Messenger, hospital tray worker
    B. Foot press operator, practical nurse
    C. Shoeshine man, barber
    D. Plumber's helper, elevator operator

18.____

19. Of the following, which one is the MOST common etiological factor in clinical cases of intellectual disability?

    A. Phenylketonuria
    B. Down syndrome
    C. Organic brain damage
    D. Environmental deprivation

19.____

20. Which of the following types of recreational activity are MOST appropriate for the intellectually disabled?

    A. Basketball, swimming
    B. Dancing, bowling
    C. Football, boxing
    D. Stickball, roller skating

20.____

KEY (CORRECT ANSWERS)

1.	B		11.	B
2.	A		12.	D
3.	C		13.	C
4.	D		14.	A
5.	D		15.	D
6.	A		16.	B
7.	B		17.	D
8.	A		18.	A
9.	D		19.	C
10.	A		20.	B

TEST 2

1. The instructional program for the intellectually disabled stresses   1.____

     A. association   B. configuration
     C. perseveration   D. habit formation

2. Of the following, the MAJOR goal of the education of disabled children is to enable them to   2.____

     A. become skilled workers in selected jobs
     B. develop a better understanding of their problems and make a better adjustment to them
     C. become completely socially adequate in their communities
     D. develop qualities of leadership in limited areas

3. The MAJOR way in which the development of the disabled child resembles that of the normal child in the early years of life is in the attainment of   3.____

     A. locomotion skills   B. manual dexterity
     C. language skills   D. physical size

4. The terminology used in characterizing the disabled has changed over the years. Which one of the following CORRECTLY gives the order in which past terms have appeared?   4.____

     A. Mentally deficient, mentally handicapped, feebleminded
     B. Mentally deficient, feebleminded, mentally retarded
     C. Feebleminded, mentally deficient, mentally retarded
     D. Mentally retarded, feebleminded, mentally deficient

5. As the severely disabled child approaches adolescence and adulthood, there is a tendency for the IQ to   5.____

     A. decline
     B. remain static
     C. show slight but positive increases
     D. show significant increases

6. When used with reference to intellectually disabled children, the term *adaptive behavior* refers to the child's   6.____

     A. ability to shift readily from one learning situation to another
     B. prognosis for anti-social behavior
     C. effectiveness in coping with the social demands of the environment
     D. functioning level as determined by a projective testing technique

7. In presenting areas of interest for the disabled adolescent: 7.____
     I. Budgeting
     II. Study of Job Areas
     III. The Worker as a Citizen and Social Being
     IV. Choosing, Getting, and Holding a Job

The MOST appropriate sequence is

     A. II, IV, I, III   B. IV, III, II, I
     C. I, II, III, IV   D. IV, I, III, II

8. Studies comparing the forgetting of completed and incomplete tasks tend to show that 8.____

    A. completed tasks tend to be forgotten more rapidly than incomplete ones
    B. incomplete tasks tend to be forgotten more rapidly than completed ones
    C. there is no difference in retention of the two types of tasks
    D. the inconclusive results that have been obtained make it impossible to generalize

9. Of the following, which is generally MOST conducive to the mastery of a skill? 9.____

    A. The practice of the skill in a daily routine
    B. Emphasis on speed rather than accuracy in early practice
    C. Overlearning
    D. Lack of emotion and pressure during practice

10. Degree of maturity, amount of previous experience, and motivation are all factors affecting the degree of _______ shown by a learner. 10.____

    A. intelligent activity   B. transfer of skills
    C. readiness   D. retention

11. Of the following, which one is of relatively minor effectiveness in determining the amount of transfer of learning from one subject to another? The 11.____

    A. degree of relationship between the two subjects involved
    B. methods used by the teacher to establish a relationship between the subjects involved
    C. amount of study time put in by the learner on the material
    D. ability of the learner to make generalizations

12. Where there are no adequate public facilities for the instruction of an intellectually disabled child who can reasonably be expected to profit from such instruction, the parent 12.____

    A. may keep the child at home until a facility becomes available
    B. may educate the child privately, deducting the costs from state and federal taxes as legitimate medical expenses
    C. may register the child in a class conducted by a parents' organization in the state, with the state paying tuition charges
    D. can apply for state aid under an appropriate section of the Education Law

13. Learning and maturation differ from one another as forms of behavior development in that the latter 13.____

    A. depends on special training during a critical period
    B. is continuous, while the former is not
    C. must be externally prompted
    D. appears spontaneously

14. The long retention of skills such as swimming is generally explained by reference to the 14.____

    A. law of multiple response
    B. law of effect
    C. effect of overlearning
    D. process of redisintegration

15. Which one of the following psychologists identified the five stages (sensorimotor opera-   15.____
tions, preconceptual thought, intuitive thought, concrete operations, and formal operations) in intellectual development?

    A. Edward L. Thorndike   B. Frances L. Ilg
    C. Jean Piaget   D. Arnold Gesell

16. A practical application of the *stimulus-response* theory of learning is BEST exemplified in   16.____
the classroom by the use of

    A. audio-visual aids
    B. experience charts
    C. developmental reading techniques
    D. teaching machines

17. Of the following, the use of the *conditioned-response* method of learning has been found   17.____
MOST successful in dealing with

    A. enuresis   B. epileptic seizures
    C. attitudes   D. reading disabilities

18. The type of forgetting in which people tend to forget the names of persons they do not   18.____
like is generally termed

    A. negative retention   B. repression
    C. proactive inhibition   D. retroactive inhibition

19. Experimental evidence suggests that the MOST effective learning and retention of mate-   19.____
rial such as poetry takes place when the material is memorized

    A. as a whole unit   B. word by word
    C. line by line   D. stanza by stanza

20. The MOST recent theories of the causation of reading disabilities stress as a major fac-   20.____
tor

    A. perceptual dysfunctions and lags
    B. lack of cultural stimulation
    C. minimal brain damage
    D. lack of parental interest and aspiration

KEY (CORRECT ANSWERS)

1.	D	11.	C
2.	B	12.	D
3.	D	13.	D
4.	C	14.	C
5.	A	15.	C
6.	C	16.	D
7.	A	17.	A
8.	A	18.	B
9.	C	19.	A
10.	C	20.	A

EXAMINATION SECTION
TEST 1

DIRECTIONS: Each question or incomplete statement is followed by several suggested answers or completions. Select the one that BEST answers the question or completes the statement. *PRINT THE LETTER OF THE CORRECT ANSWER IN THE SPACE AT THE RIGHT.*

1. An effective method to correct mirror writing by the intellectually disabled is to   1._____

    A. have him write looking through a mirror
    B. have him change from use of left hand to the right hand
    C. re-emphasize the correct posture and position for writing
    D. have him copy models showing the starting point of writing

2. Dr. Robert Guthrie developed a blood test to be administered to infants to detect the presence of   2._____

    A. syphilis   B. hypothyroidism
    C. hydrocephalus   D. phenylketonuria

3. Which of the following defines intellectual disability as a disability characterized by significant limitations both in intellectual functioning and in adaptive behavior, originating before age 18 and covering a range of everyday social and practical skills?   3._____

    A. American Association on Intellectual and Developmental Disabilities
    B. E.A. Doll
    C. Council for Exceptional Children
    D. Clemens Benda

4. Early studies on the nature of intelligence revealed that the BEST predictors of intelligence for school-age children were _______ tasks.   4._____

    A. simple sensori-motor   B. complex sensori-motor
    C. speed of reaction to timed   D. complex verbal

5. Which of the following conditions automatically warrants the exclusion of intellectually disabled children from school attendance?   5._____

    A. Lack of toilet training   B. Petit-mal epilepsy
    C. Aphasia   D. Anxiety

6. Which one of the following state agencies is assigned the responsibility for carrying out planning in intellectual disablities? Department of   6._____

    A. Education   B. Welfare
    C. Labor   D. Mental Hygiene

7. Which one of the following publications dealt exclusively with intellectual disablity and related problems?   7._____

    A. THE VOLTA REVIEW
    B. THE TRAINING SCHOOL BULLETIN
    C. EXCEPTIONAL CHILDREN
    D. THE JOURNAL OF GENETIC PSYCHOLOGY

8. *It is just as important to integrate the mentally retarded within our society and make full use of their abilities as it is to make a special effort to do this for the physically handicapped.*
This statement was made by

    A. John F. Kennedy
    B. Lyndon B. Johnson
    C. Hubert Humphrey
    D. Dwight D. Eisenhower

9. The study of mental deficiency as a specialized branch of medicine did NOT develop until

    A. Itard demonstrated his success with the Wild Boy of Aveyron
    B. investigators realized that mental defect required treatment dissimilar to that of mental illness
    C. Goddard's work on the inheritance of mental defect was published
    D. Pinel removed the shackles from the patients at the Hospice des Bicetre

10. The *patterning* method of treating neurologically handicapped children was originated at the Institute

    A. of Neurological Diseases
    B. for the Achievement of Human Potential
    C. of Defectology
    D. for the Crippled and Disabled

11. Which one of the following may properly be considered the MOST significant recent development in rehabilitation of the intellectually disabled? The

    A. use of new diagnostic techniques with disabled young adults
    B. development of combined school-work programs
    C. use of rehabilitation counselors in the schools
    D. identification of social problems of the intellectually disabled

12. Which one of the following needs of the intellectually disabled is often minimized?

    A. Diagnosis
    B. Institutionalization
    C. Development of worthwhile leisure time activities
    D. Specially trained teachers

13. Which of the following is the MOST likely underlying cause of most vandalism in intellectually disabled school-age children?

    A. Compensation for feelings of helplessness
    B. Inadequate protection of property
    C. Delinquent or pre-delinquent personality structure
    D. Intra-gang competitiveness

14. Of the following, the developer of the *talking typewriter* used with disabled children was

    A. Samuel A. Kirk
    B. Albert J. Harris
    C. Paul A. Witty
    D. Omar K. Moore

15. The leaders in the national campaign to treat intellectual disablity recommend that the major responsibility for development of programs should be assumed by   15.____

    A. the federal government   B. community agencies
    C. state governments   D. municipal governments

16. A recent development in post-school vocational placement of the intellectually disabled is the assignment of the responsibility for placement to   16.____

    A. guidance counselors of the Board of Education's special education department
    B. community offices of the State Employment Service
    C. selective placement counselors of the Division of Vocational Rehabilitation
    D. special committees functioning within the parent organizations for the disabled

17. Which one of the following is a suitable industrial job operation for which a disabled high school student may be trained?   17.____

    A. Wire preparation and soldering
    B. Hot water boiler assembly
    C. Steamfitting
    D. Repair work on electric and gas driven lawnmowers

18. The PRIME objective of an educational program for the intellectually disabled should be the development of   18.____

    A. avocational pursuits and hobbies to fill their leisure time
    B. manipulative ability that will lead to some marketable skills
    C. reading skills that include the basic words in *reading for protection*
    D. general communication skills in both the school and the home

19. In a program of occupational education for the intellectually disabled, vocational guidance is interpreted as encompassing   19.____

    A. a study of appropriate jobs
    B. help for those with limited vocational potential to find jobs
    C. self-evaluation of individual qualifications against specific job requirements
    D. job placement

20. The average lifespan of an individual with Down syndrome is closest to   20.____

    A. 25   B. 35   C. 50   D. 60

KEY (CORRECT ANSWERS)

1.	D	11.	B
2.	D	12.	C
3.	A	13.	A
4.	D	14.	D
5.	A	15.	C
6.	D	16.	B
7.	B	17.	A
8.	A	18.	D
9.	B	19.	C
10.	B	20.	D

TEST 2

DIRECTIONS: Each question or incomplete statement is followed by several suggested answers or completions. Select the one that BEST answers the question or completes the statement. *PRINT THE LETTER OF THE CORRECT ANSWER IN THE SPACE AT THE RIGHT.*

1. In this state, the period of compulsory school attendance for intellectually disabled children is

    A. the same as that for non-disabled children
    B. shorter than that for non-disabled children
    C. longer than that for non-disabled children
    D. either shorter or longer than that for non-disabled children, depending on the child's actual class progress

    1.____

2. Recent publications from the federal government estimate the number of intellectually disabled people in the country to be APPROXIMATELY ______ million.

    A. 2.5   B. 6.5   C. 8.5   D. 11.5

    2.____

3. A MOST significant legislative event relative to intellectual disablity was the passage of a law

    A. making it mandatory that all infants be tested for phenylketonuria
    B. subsidizing sheltered workshops on a per capita basis
    C. making it mandatory that emotionally disturbed children be provided with educational programs
    D. providing a salary differential for teachers of handicapped children

    3.____

4. Which one of the following individuals exerted the GREATEST influence in the training of disabled children?

    A. Piaget   B. Montessori   C. Freud   D. Seguin

    4.____

5. The incidence of intellectual disablity is

    A. greater among males than females
    B. greater among the offspring of the poor than the rich
    C. proportionally greater among Black than among white families
    D. greater among the offspring of uneducated than among offspring of educated families

    5.____

6. The qualifying conditions for intellectual disablity for different age groups include social adjustment, learning ability, and rate of maturation.
Rate of maturation as a factor in intellectual disablity has special significance during the

    A. first few years of life   B. primary school years
    C. adolescent period   D. young adult period

    6.____

7. Rubella may cause intellectual disablity when contracted by a pregnant woman, particularly during the

    A. first three months of pregnancy
    B. second three months of pregnancy
    C. third three months of pregnancy
    D. latter half of the pregnancy period

    7.____

8. Studies of the relative abilities of disabled and normal individuals in learning indicate that the intellectually disabled
    8.____

    A. show no difference in the rate or amount of learning compared to their normal peers of the same mental age
    B. are less capable in abstracting and generalizing from their experiences
    C. are not affected by the complexity of the task presented
    D. cannot be trained to use verbal cues in learning

9. Which one of the following phases of the Occupational Education program is NOT the responsibility of the teacher?
    9.____

    A. Occupational information
    B. Vocational guidance
    C. Job placement
    D. Vocational training

10. A program of Occupational Education for the disabled adolescent places GREATEST emphasis upon the development of
    10.____

    A. personal-social
    B. social-occupational
    C. occupational-academic
    D. academic-personal

11. In a program of Occupational Education for the intellectually disabled, vocational training should emphasize MOST heavily training in
    11.____

    A. non-manual skills necessary in the work area
    B. general habits, attitudes, and skills common to good workmanship and citizenship
    C. manual skills needed in the work area
    D. measuring individual abilities against job requirements

12. In general, the HIGHEST job level at which an intellectually disabled individual can function in open competitive industry is as a(n)
    12.____

    A. sheltered helper
    B. skilled worker
    C. semi-skilled worker
    D. unskilled worker

13. Which one of the following is the PRIMARY objective of the Work-Study program for intellectually disabled youth?
    13.____

    A. Developing a realistic attitude toward school
    B. Determining the types of jobs they will be qualified to hold
    C. Emphasizing proper job attitudes
    D. Helping pupils make a successful transition from school to full-time employment

14. MOST maladoptive behavior of the intellectually disabled child is a function of his
    14.____

    A. disablity
    B. interpersonal relationships
    C. academic frustrations
    D. faulty perception of the environment

15. The emotional problems exhibited by intellectually disabled children are essentially
    15.____

    A. the same kind as those exhibited by non-disabled children
    B. dependent primarily upon the clinical classification of disablity
    C. determined by the child's constitutional endowment
    D. qualitatively different from those of children who are not disabled

16. The BEST single diagnostic index of disablity in a young pre-school child with normal visual and auditory capacities is   16.____

    A. an underdeveloped comprehension and speaking vocabulary for his age
    B. delayed motor development for his age
    C. inability to distinguish stimuli simultaneously presented to the face and hand
    D. an abnormal EEG record

17. According to Stanford-Binet, an IQ between 55 and 69 is ______ impaired or delayed.   17.____

    A. severely   B. moderately   C. mildly   D. average

18. Down syndrome is associated with   18.____

    A. head trauma   B. chromosomes   C. nutrition   D. infection

19. Which one of the following is MOST likely to be symptomatic of the defense mechanism known as *regression* in an older disabled child?   19.____

    A. Sudden immature behavior in a class
    B. Constant *forgetting* to do a class assignment
    C. Affirming that a dead parent is still alive
    D. Acting like another well-liked child in the class

20. To which one of the following therapeutic techniques is the use of role playing as a guidance tool MOST closely related?   20.____

    A. Group therapy   B. Free association
    C. Psychotherapy   D. Psychodrama

KEY (CORRECT ANSWERS)

1.	A	11.	B
2.	B	12.	C
3.	A	13.	D
4.	D	14.	B
5.	A	15.	A
6.	A	16.	A
7.	A	17.	C
8.	B	18.	B
9.	C	19.	A
10.	B	20.	D

———

EXAMINATION SECTION
TEST 1

DIRECTIONS: Each question or incomplete statement is followed by several suggested answers or completions. Select the one that BEST answers the question or completes the statement. *PRINT THE LETTER OF THE CORRECT ANSWER IN THE SPACE AT THE RIGHT.*

1. The causes of abnormal behavior include

    A. alcohol and drugs
    B. head injuries and severe infection
    C. diabetes and psychiatric problems
    D. all of the above

1.____

2. All of the following are common reactions to anxiety EXCEPT

    A. depression
    B. flight of ideas
    C. denial
    D. regression

2.____

3. Of the following infections, the one which does NOT produce psychotic syndrome is

    A. chancroid
    B. brain abscess
    C. syphilis
    D. toxoplasmosis

3.____

4. In dealing with emotionally disturbed patients, an EMT should

    A. not assess the patient's needs
    B. intervene in the situation to the extent to which he feels capable
    C. overreact to the patient's behavior or emotional attacks
    D. none of the above

4.____

5. Crisis situations, including periods of ______, may affect the paramedic adversely.

    A. anxiety
    B. anger
    C. impatience
    D. all of the above

5.____

6. A professional attitude MUST be maintained while the paramedic is dealing with emotionally disturbed patients. This attitude can be characterized by all of the following EXCEPT

    A. anger
    B. warmth
    C. sensitivity
    D. compassion

6.____

7. The common emotional difficulties of the paramedic may be managed by

    A. discussing problems and anxieties with co-workers
    B. developing a regular discussion rap session with peers to discuss good and bad experiences
    C. discussing problems with the supervisor
    D. all of the above

7.____

8. There are certain general guidelines for dealing with any patient with a psychiatric problem.
The one of the following which is NOT among these guidelines is:

   A. Be prepared to spend time with the disturbed patient.
   B. Be as calm and direct as possibl
   C. You do not need to identify yoursel
   D. Assess the patient wherever the emergency occurs.

9. Disorders of motor activity include all of the following EXCEPT

   A. agitation   B. compulsion
   C. perservation   D. restlessness

10. A repetitive action carried out to relieve the anxiety of obsessive thought is called

   A. compulsion   B. delirium
   C. confrontation   D. confabulation

11. The invention of experiences to cover over gaps in memory, seen in patients with certain organic brain syndromes, is

   A. dementia   B. confabulation
   C. psychosis   D. delusion

12. Among the following, which is NOT a symptom of a panic attack?

   A. Shortness of breath or a sensation of being smothered
   B. Feeling of unreality or of stepping apart from oneself
   C. Constant fatigue and no motivation to do anything
   D. Fear of dying and of being crazy

13. Risk factors for violence do NOT include

   A. any place where alcohol is being consumed
   B. natural death in the family
   C. crowd incidents
   D. incidents where violence has already occurred (e.g., shooting, stabbing)

14. Disorders of thinking include all of the following EXCEPT

   A. flight of ideas   B. retardation of thought
   C. compulsions   D. perseveration

15. All of the following are disorders of consciousness EXCEPT

   A. amnesia   B. delirium
   C. fugue stage   D. stupor and coma

16. A repetition of movements that don,t seem to serve any useful purpose is called

   A. compulsion   B. echolalia
   C. stereotyped activity   D. all of the above

8.___
9.___
10.___
11.___
12.___
13.___
14.___
15.___
16.___

17. The definition of *compulsion* is: 17.____

    A. A repetitive action carried out to relieve the anxiety of obsessive thought
    B. The situation in which a patient cannot sit still
    C. Condition in which the patient echoes the words of the examiner
    D. None of the above

18. The MOST profound disorder of memory is   18.____

    A. confabulation   B. amnesia
    C. illusion   D. hallucination

19. An acute state of confusion characterized by global impairment of thinking, perception,   19.____
and memory is called

    A. delusion   B. delirium   C. psychosis   D. dementia

20. Proper pre-hospital management of the manic patient includes   20.____

    A. not arguing or getting into a power struggle with the patient
    B. talking to a patient in a quiet place, away from other people
    C. consulting medical command if the patient refuses transport
    D. all of the above

Questions 21-25.

DIRECTIONS: In Questions 21 through 25, match the numbered definition with the lettered
                    disorder, listed in Column I, that it MOST accurately describes. Place the letter
                    of the CORRECT answer in the appropriate space at the right.

<u>COLUMN I</u>
A. Echolalia
B. Illusion
C. Delusion
D. Hallucination
E. Mood

21. Misinterpretation of sensory stimuli   21.____

22. False belief   22.____

23. Meaningless echoing of the interviewer's words by the patient   23.____

24. Sustained and pervasive emotional state   24.____

25. Sense of perception not founded on objective reality   25.____

KEY (CORRECT ANSWERS)

1.	D	11.	B
2.	B	12.	C
3.	A	13.	B
4.	B	14.	C
5.	D	15.	A
6.	A	16.	C
7.	D	17.	A
8.	C	18.	B
9.	C	19.	B
10.	A	20.	D

21.	B
22.	C
23.	A
24.	E
25.	D

TEST 2

DIRECTIONS: Each question or incomplete statement is followed by several suggested answers or completions. Select the one that BEST answers the question or completes the statement. *PRINT THE LETTER OF THE CORRECT ANSWER IN THE SPACE AT THE RIGHT.*

1. The depressed patient can often be readily identified by   1._____

    A. a sad expression
    B. bouts of crying
    C. expression of feelings of worthlessness
    D. all of the above

2. The third leading cause of death among the 15- to 25 year-old age group is   2._____

    A. diabetes mellitus   B. rheumatoid arthritis
    C. suicide   D. congenital heart disease

3. The assessment of every depressed person MUST include an evaluation of   3._____

    A. schizophrenia
    B. suicide risk
    C. chronic debilitating illness
    D. anxiety

4. When caring for a patient who is displaying typical stress reactions, you should   4._____

    A. act in a calm manner, giving the patient time to gain control of his emotions
    B. quietly and carefully evaluate the situation
    C. stay alert for sudden changes in behavior
    D. all of the above

5. The patient in a psychiatric emergency is far more out of reach and out of control than the person in an emotional emergency.   5._____
    In a psychiatric emergency, the patient may do all of the following EXCEPT

    A. try to hurt himself
    B. try to seek help for protection
    C. withdraw, no longer responding to people or to his environment
    D. continue to act depressed, sometimes crying and expressing feelings of worthlessness

6. When a patient is acting as if he may hurt himself or another, you should do all of the following EXCEPT   6._____

    A. alert the police
    B. not isolate yourself from your partner or other sources of help
    C. try to restrain the patient by yourself
    D. always be on the watch for weapons

7. A mental disorder characterized by loss of contact with reality is called   7._____

    A. psychosis   B. dementia
    C. phobia   D. none of the above

8. Anti-psychotic drugs are also called 8.____

   A. antidepressants   B. neuroleptics
   C. anxiolytics   D. antiepileptics

9. The patient who hears voices commanding him to hurt himself or others must be considered 9.____

   A. normal   B. safe
   C. dangerous   D. none of the above

10. When in a state of *conversion hysteria,* a person's 10.____

   A. reaction may move from extreme anxiety to relative calmness
   B. may transform anxiety to some bodily function
   C. often becomes hysterically blind, deaf, or paralyzed
   D. all of the above

11. Repeating the same idea over and over again is called 11.____

   A. perseveration   B. compulsion
   C. obsession   D. facilitation

12. ______ is the interviewing technique in which the interviewer encourages the patient to proceed by noncommittal words and gestures. 12.____

   A. Echolalia   B. Facilitation
   C. Affect   D. None of the above

13. The CHRONIC deterioration of mental function is referred to as 13.____

   A. dementia   B. psychosis
   C. delirium   D. schizophrenia

14. A persistent idea that a person CANNOT dismiss from his thought is a(n) 14.____

   A. affect   B. obsession
   C. compulsion   D. delusion

15. An interviewing technique in which the interviewer points out to the patient something of interest in his conversa tion or behavior is 15.____

   A. facilitation   B. confabulation
   C. confrontation   D. perseveration

16. It is important for paramedics to be aware of one particular syndrome that may occur in patients taking anti-psychotic medication.
This condition is 16.____

   A. acute diuresis   B. acute dystonic reaction
   C. hypertensive crises   D. none of the above

17. An acute dystonic reaction can be rapidly corrected by 17.____

   A. chlorpromazine   B. prolixin
   C. diphenhydramine   D. tindal

18. Tranquilizers are also called   18.____

    A. neuroleptics   B. anxiolytics
    C. chinergics   D. stimulants

19. The COMMON symptoms of antipsychotic drugs include   19.____

    A. blurred vision   B. dry mouth
    C. cardiac dysrhythmias   D. all of the above

20. Uncontrolled, disconnected thoughts characterize a dis organized patient who may be   20.____

    A. incoherent or rambling in his speech
    B. wandering aimlessly
    C. dressed inappropriately
    D. all of the above

Questions 21-25.

DIRECTIONS: In Questions 21 through 25, match the numbered definition with the lettered disorder, listed in Column I, that it MOST accurately describes. Place the letter of the CORRECT answer in the appropriate space at the right.

<u>COLUMN I</u>
    A. Agitation
    B. Agoraphobia
    C. Flight of ideas
    D. Neologism
    E. Confabulation

21. Fear of the marketplace   21.____

22. An invented word that has meaning only to its inventor   22.____

23. The invention of experiences to cover over gaps in memory   23.____

24. Extreme restlessness and anxiety   24.____

25. Accelerated thinking in which the mind skips very rapidly from one thought to the next   25.____

KEY (CORRECT ANSWERS)

1.	D	11.	A
2.	C	12.	B
3.	B	13.	A
4.	D	14.	B
5.	B	15.	C
6.	C	16.	B
7.	A	17.	C
8.	B	18.	B
9.	C	19.	D
10.	D	20.	D

21.	B
22.	D
23.	E
24.	A
25.	C

EXAMINATION SECTION
TEST 1

DIRECTIONS: Each question or incomplete statement is followed by several suggested answers or completions. Select the one that BEST answers the question or completes the statement. *PRINT THE LETTER OF THE CORRECT ANSWER IN THE SPACE AT THE RIGHT.*

1. A relationship in which a patient becomes dependent on the nurse   1.____

   A. is always unprofessional
   B. is inevitably "bad" for the patient
   C. may be necessary temporarily
   D. impedes learning

2. Anxiety is the CHIEF characteristic of the   2.____

   A. immature personality
   B. psychoneurotic disorder
   C. involutional psychotic reaction
   D. mentally retarded adolescent

3. The mode of psychological adjustment known as regression can BEST be described as   3.____

   A. refusing to think of unpleasant situations
   B. changing to a type of behavior which is characteristic of an earlier period in life
   C. reverting to actions characteristic of an historically early or primitive code of behavior
   D. hostility towards persons or objects that prove frustrating

4. The CHIEF danger in the employment of escape mechanisms as a form of adjustment is that they   4.____

   A. do more harm than good
   B. are socially undesirable
   C. make the experience expensive
   D. leave the basic problem unsolved

5. In essential hypertension, there is a(n)   5.____

   A. *increase* in systolic pressure and a *decrease* in diastolic pressure
   B. *decrease* in systolic pressure and an *increase* in diastolic pressure
   C. *increase* in *both* systolic and diastolic pressure
   D. *decrease* in *both* systolic and diastolic pressure

6. The *initial* paralysis in cerebral vascular accident, regardless of cause, is the type known as   6.____

   A. spastic   B. paraplegic   C. flaccid   D. rigid

7. Cerebral hemorrhage *most frequently* occurs in males in the age range from   7.____

   A. 20 to 30 years   B. 30 to 40 years
   C. 40 to 50 years   D. 50 years and over

8. Hereditary progressive muscular dystrophy is a disease characterized by progressive   8.____
    weakness and final atrophy of groups of muscles.
    Of the following statements about muscular dystrophy, the one which is LEAST accu-
    rate is that

    A. there is no known cure for muscular dystrophy at present
    B. muscular dystrophy is a disease of the central nervous system
    C. early signs of muscular dystrophy are frequent falls, difficulty climbing stairs, devel-
        opment of lordosis, and a waddling gait
    D. therapeutic exercises may have some temporary value in the treatment of muscu-
        lar dystrophy

9. The home care program is an extension of the hospital's service into the home on an   9.____
    extra-mural basis.
    Of the following statements, the one that BEST explains the success of this program is
    that it

    A. *recognizes* the value to the patient and his family of the preservation of normal
        family life despite the limitations imposed by the patient's illness
    B. *makes* more hospital beds available for acute illnesses and emergency care
    C. reduces the cost of hospital care by reducing the number of inpatients
    D. *simplifies* hospital administration by reducing the number of chronically ill in hospi-
        tals

10. The MOST important of the following reasons for the rehabilitation of the seriously hand-   10.____
    icapped individual is that

    A. hospitalization of the handicapped is usually prolonged and costly to the commu-
        nity
    B. beds occupied by such patients reduce the number of hospital beds available for
        acutely ill patients
    C. care of chronically ill or handicapped patients is taxing and difficult for the family,
        the nurse, and the doctor
    D. it is important to the patient that he be as independent and useful as possible

11. There has been a notable increase in the discharge rate from mental institutions in the   11.____
    state during recent years. This change in statistics may be attributed CHIEFLY to

    A. increasing use of psychoanalysis and better trained personnel
    B. new drugs, changes in admission procedures, and the "open door" policy
    C. the increase in nursing homes for the elderly
    D. the use of psychotherapeutics and early diagnosis of mental illness

12. The PRINCIPAL and BASIC objective of mental hygiene is to   12.____

    A. modify attitudes as well as unhealthy behavior secondary to unhealthy attitudes
    B. care for the post-hospitalized psychiatric patient at home
    C. increase mental hygiene clinic services
    D. stimulate interest in improved education for doctors, nurses, and teachers

13. Separation of a child from his own home and placement in a foster home often arouses 13.____
adverse reactions in the child. Of the following, the one which is MOST serious for the
child is

    A. homesickness
    B. withdrawn behavior
    C. rebellion against authority
    D. dislike of new people

14. Behavior problems of the adolescent school child can BEST be explained by the fact that 14.____

    A. the adolescent suddenly becomes aware of the opposite sex at this time
    B. the demands made on adolescents by intolerant parents create rebellion against
authority
    C. during childhood there is a general disregard of the child's need for independence
by parents and other adults
    D. adolescence is a transition period between childhood and adulthood which usually
creates feelings of insecurity in the adolescent

15. Of the following, the behavior which is LEAST indicative of serious emotional maladjust- 15.____
ment in an adolescent boy is

    A. lying and cheating   B. shyness and daydreaming
    C. gross overweight   D. association with a teen-age gang

16. The one of the following diseases which is caused by a birth injury is 16.____

    A. cerebral palsy   B. meningitis
    C. hydrocele   D. congenital syphilis
    E. epilepsy

17. A delusion is a 17.____

    A. disharmony of mind and body
    B. fantastic image formed during sleep
    C. false judgment of objective things
    D. cessation of thought
    E. distorted perception or image

18. The one of the following which is the MOST common form of treatment employed by 18.____
psychiatrists in treating patients with mental disorders is

    A. hypnotism   B. hydrotherapy
    C. electroshock   D. insulin shock
    E. psychotherapy

19. A masochistic person is one who 19.____

    A. is very melancholy
    B. has delusions of grandeur about himself
    C. derives pleasure from being cruelly treated
    D. believes in a fatalistic philosophy
    E. derives pleasure from hurting another

20. Surgery is *ESPECIALLY* difficult during the Oedipal period because of the   20.____

   A. father attachment   B. mental age
   C. castration anxieties   D. rejection complex
   E. separation from siblings

21. A psychometric test is one which attempts to measure   21.____

   A. social adjustment   B. emotional maturity
   C. physical activity   D. personality development
   E. Intellectual capacity

22. The one of the following conditions which falls into the classification of a psychosis   22.____
rather than psychoneurosis is

   A. anxiety hysteria   B. schizophrenia
   C. neurasthenia   D. convesion hysteria
   E. compulsion neurosis

23. The one of the following which BEST describes psychosomatic medicine is: 23.____

   A. The understanding and treatment of both mind and body in illness
   B. The treatment of disease by psychiatric methods only
   C. The separation of mind and body in medical treatment
   D. The psychological testing of all individuals
   E. A system of socialized medical planning

24. The one of the following conditions for which shock treatment is *FREQUENTLY* used is   24.____

   A. alcoholism   B. Parkinson's syndrome
   C. multiple sclerosis   D. schizophrenia
   E. diabetes

25. The one of the following conditions which is *NOT* caused by the dysfunction of endo-   25.____
crine glands is

   A. myxedema   B. duodenal ulcer
   C. cretinism   D. Addison's disease
   E. none of the above

KEY (CORRECT ANSWERS)

1.	C		11.	B
2.	B		12.	A
3.	B		13.	B
4.	D		14.	D
5.	C		15.	D
6.	C		16.	A
7.	D		17.	C
8.	B		18.	E
9.	A		19.	C
10.	D		20.	C

21.	E
22.	B
23.	A
24.	D
25.	B

TEST 2

DIRECTIONS: Each question or incomplete statement is followed by several suggested answers or completions. Select the one that BEST answers the question or completes the statement. *PRINT THE LETTER OF THE CORRECT ANSWER IN THE SPACE AT THE RIGHT.*

1. Euphoria is a state of   1.____

    A. depression   B. elation   C. ideation   D. frustration

2. An ailment found only in older people is   2.____

    A. manic depression   B. dementia praecox
    C. senile dementia   D. tabes dorsalis

3. The permissive policy employed in some mental hospitals is associated with a(n)   3.____

    A. increase in assaultive behavior
    B. open door policy
    C. decrease in the use of physical restraint
    D. increase in the use of physical restraint

4. A symptom of dementia praecox is   4.____

    A. extroversion   B. tic paralysis
    C. unpredictability   D. cerebral hemorrhage

5. Substituting an activity in which a person can succeed for one in which he may fail is   5.____

    A. sublimation   B. projection
    C. rationalization   D. compensation

6. Rationalization is the result of   6.____

    A. believing what one wants to believe
    B. reflective thinking
    C. scientific thinking
    D. basing conclusions on fact

7. Delusions of persecution are typical of   7.____

    A. epilepsy   B. regression
    C. schizophrenia   D. paranoia

8. A person with an IQ of 85 would be classified as   8.____

    A. defective   B. normal
    C. dull average   D. borderline

9. The term describing physical symptoms that do not arise *ENTIRELY* from physical causes is   9.____

    A. organic   B. psychoneurotic
    C. psychosomatic   D. psychopathological

10. The mechanism of attributing one's own ideas to others is termed   10._____

    A. projection   B. substitution
    C. sublimation   D. rationalization

11. A child's tendency to pattern after his parents is known as   11._____

    A. identification   B. projection
    C. compensation   D. substitution

12. Stuttering in children *USUALLY* originates from   12._____

    A. physical handicap   B. mentally deficient parents
    C. emotional handicap   D. imitation of other stutterers

13. Acute intoxication may *PROPERLY* be labeled a psychosis because it involves   13._____

    A. intellectual limitations
    B. emotional inadequacies
    C. bodily disease
    D. a severe loss of contact with reality

14. The outstanding change, of the following, in the aging process is that the aged are   14._____

    A. irritable   B. no longer self-reliant
    C. senile   D. easily influenced by stress

15. Re-adjusting the older person to be somewhat self-sufficient is known as   15._____

    A. stabilization   B. regeneration
    C. rejuvenation   D. rehabilitation

16. The spastic child usually   16._____

    A. is mentally retarded   B. is potentially schizophrenic
    C. requires speech training   D. has poor vision

17. Insomnia refers to   17._____

    A. unconsciousness   B. sleeplessness
    C. sleep walking   D. insensibility

18. A drug recently introduced in the treatment of mental illness is   18._____

    A. streptomycin   B. paramino-salicylic acid
    C. reserpine   D. cortisone

19. In general, the sleep requirement for an aged person as compared to the sleep require-   19._____
ment for a young adult is

    A. less   B. more   C. the same   D. slightly greater

20. The *MOST IMPORTANT* aspect of the rehabilitation of a person who has suffered a   20._____
stroke is the

    A. patient's emotional reaction to self
    B. doctor's attitude toward the patient
    C. nurse's attitude toward the patient
    D. family reaction toward the patient

21. If a patient tells a nurse that he is contemplating committing suicide, the nurse should

    A. not pay any attention, since people who threaten suicide seldom follow through
    B. urge him to consult a psychiatrist, since potential suicides need psychiatric help immediately
    C. be sympathetic. Her sympathy will divert him from his intention
    D. realize that he is a neurotic with whom she will try to work

21.____

22. The BEST advice you can give parents disturbed by their five-year-old child's habit of nailbiting is to tell them to

    A. find out what some of the pressures on the child are and try to relieve them
    B. paint the child's fingers with the product "bitter aloes"
    C. point out to the child that this is a baby habit and not desirable in a school child
    D. punish the child by not allowing him to watch television or go to the movies

22.____

23. In certain periods of development, anti-social behavior in young children is considered normal. However, of the following situations, the one which merits referral to a mental hygiene clinic is where

    A. a two-year-old persists in hitting his four- year-old brother
    B. a three-year-old develops enuresis when a new baby is brought into the home
    C. a four-year-old runs away from home at every opportunity
    D. a six-year-old is not friendly, has no "pals" after six months in school, and partici-pates in activities only when compelled to

23.____

24. Learning occurs

    A. when the child's responses are adequate
    B. when a solution to the situation is obvious
    C. when the adult solves the problems
    D. None of the above

24.____

25. The *FIRST* emotions to become differentiated may be described as

    A. anger and fear   B. anger and distress
    C. fear and delight   D. delight and distress

25.____

KEY (CORRECT ANSWERS)

1.	B		11.	A
2.	C		12.	C
3.	B		13.	D
4.	C		14.	D
5.	D		15.	D
6.	A		16.	C
7.	D		17.	B
8.	C		18.	C
9.	C		19.	A
10.	A		20.	A

21.	B
22.	A
23.	D
24.	A
25.	D

EXAMINATION SECTION
TEST 1

DIRECTIONS: Each question or incomplete statement is followed by several suggested answers or completions. Select the one that BEST answers the question or completes the statement. *PRINT THE LETTER OF THE CORRECT ANSWER IN THE SPACE AT THE RIGHT.*

1. Epilepsy is MAINLY associated with 1.____
   - A. brain injury
   - B. migraine
   - C. dysrhythmia
   - D. aggressivity

2. A disturbance of language perception and expression is called 2.____
   - A. aphasia B. amnesia C. amentia D. alexia

3. Alcoholism is MOST commonly connected with 3.____
   - A. dysrhythmia
   - B. neurosis
   - C. psychopathy
   - D. overt homosexuality

4. The polygraph is MOST useful for diagnosing 4.____
   - A. epilepsy
   - B. aggressivity
   - C. deception
   - D. brain damage

5. The electroencephalogram is MOST useful for diagnosing 5.____
   - A. brain tumor
   - B. epilepsy
   - C. brain injury
   - D. mental deficiency

6. Shock therapy was recommended for 6.____
   - A. paranoid schizophrenics
   - B. depressed psychotics
   - C. severe psychoneurotics
   - D. psychopaths

7. Prefrontal lobotomy had been recommended for 7.____
   - A. aggressive psychotics
   - B. apathetic psychotics
   - C. paranoid psychotics
   - D. psychopaths

8. Most authorities believe that mental deficiency is ______ hereditary. 8.____
   - A. never B. always C. sometimes D. rarely

9. Recent experiments utilizing glutamic acid in an attempt to raise the intellectual level of retarded children have resulted in 9.____
   - A. inconclusive findings
   - B. a marked temporary rise in intellectual level
   - C. a marked permanent rise in intellectual level
   - D. a slight temporary decline in intellectual level

10. An individual's Rorschach protocol may be MOST profitably interpreted in the light of his 10.____
   - A. behavior while being tested
   - B. case history
   - C. other test results
   - D. presenting problems

11. If a child is mentally retarded, his academic potential can be explained MOST readily to his parent in terms of the status of other children

    A. in his class   B. of similar CA
    C. of similar MA   D. of similar IQ

11.____

12. It is MOST probable that a school-age child characterized, on the basis of psychological tests, as a mental defective might, in fact, be

    A. epileptic   B. deaf
    C. mute   D. schizophrenic

12.____

13. The classroom behavior MOST characteristic of the brain injured child includes

    A. distractibility, hyperactivity, and lack of inhibition
    B. listlessness, withdrawal, and compulsiveness
    C. aggressiveness, fearfulness, and egocentrism
    D. perseveration, fatigue, and apathy

13.____

14. A child's MOST rapid rate of mental growth generally occurs

    A. during the first few months of life
    B. between the ages of 3-6
    C. between the ages of 6-12
    D. during early adolescence

14.____

15. A psychopath may be distinguished by the fact that he commits antisocial acts

    A. consistently
    B. without customary reaction to guilt
    C. without awareness of what he is doing
    D. violently

15.____

16. Of the following techniques, the one which is considered to be characteristic of non-directive or client-centered therapy is

    A. encouraging transference
    B. reflection of feeling
    C. free association
    D. permissive questioning

16.____

17. Psychoanalytic writers consider the MOST important aspect of an analyst's training to be his

    A. training in psychoanalytic concepts
    B. training in medicine
    C. training in analysis
    D. general psychological training

17.____

18. In the transference situation, it is MOST probable that there will be ______ feeling(s) between analyst and patient.

    A. positive   B. negative
    C. neutral   D. positive and negative

18.____

19. The sequelae of encephalitis   19.____

    A.   are now preventable in virtually every case of the disease
    B.   may become evident long after an acute attack of the disease
    C.   respond readily to treatment when detected
    D.   are physical and emotional but rarely mental

20. The mental mechanism most strongly EMPHASIZED in psychoanalytic formulations of   20.____
schizophrenia is

    A.   repression   B.   conversion
    C.   projection   D.   regression

21. Paranoia differs from the paranoid type of schizophrenia in   21.____

    A.   the occurrence of delusions in one and not the other
    B.   the fact that the paranoid patient does not act on the basis of his delusions
    C.   the amount of *psychopathic tainting* in the family history
    D.   that the delusions are more systematized

22. According to the Freudian psychoanalysts, the personality changes in general paresis   22.____
are due to

    A.   oedipus complex   B.   infantile sex urges
    C.   sublimations   D.   changes in narcissism

23. A patient who touched his chin when asked to touch his nose would be MOST likely to be   23.____
suffering from

    A.   motor apraxia   B.   motor ataxia
    C.   sensory apraxia   D.   agnosia

24. Shock treatment for schizophrenia, especially by the use of metrazol, was introduced at   24.____
first because of the theory that

    A.   shock arouses special physiological defense mechanisms by way of the *alarm
reaction*
    B.   shock stimulates the autonomic nervous sytem and thus facilitates homeostasis
    C.   convulsions protect epileptics against developing schizophrenic symptoms
    D.   shock as a form of punishment gratifies the patient's masochistic tendencies

25. From his survey of experimental evidence on the effect of infant care on later personality,   25.____
Orlansky was led to the conclusion that such factors as breastfeeding and toilet-training

    A.   are of no significance for later personality
    B.   are significant determiners of personality
    C.   are relevant to personality only insofar as they indicate the mother's attitude, which
is the effective factor
    D.   may help determine personality but constitutional and post-infantile factors should
receive major emphasis

———

KEY (CORRECT ANSWERS)

1.	C		11.	C
2.	A		12.	D
3.	B		13.	A
4.	C		14.	A
5.	B		15.	B
6.	B		16.	B
7.	A		17.	C
8.	C		18.	D
9.	A		19.	B
10.	B		20.	D

21.	D
22.	D
23.	A
24.	C
25.	D

TEST 2

DIRECTIONS: Each question or incomplete statement is followed by several suggested answers or completions. Select the one that BEST answers the question or completes the statement. *PRINT THE LETTER OF THE CORRECT ANSWER IN THE SPACE AT THE RIGHT.*

1. A part of the nervous system NOT known to have any connection with emotional behavior is referred to as the   1.____

    A.   parasympathetic nervous system
    B.   basal ganglia
    C.   frontal lobes of cerebral cortex
    D.   temporal lobes of cerebral cortex

2. A phobia is _______ anxiety.   2.____

    A.   less specific than   B.   more specific than
    C.   synonymous with an   D.   less acute than

3. The division of the autonomic nervous system that coordinates bodily changes in fear and anger is   3.____

    A.   sacral   B.   sympathetic
    C.   emergency   D.   cranial

4. The effect of familiarity in the case of inter-racial attitudes is   4.____

    A.   dependent upon the nature of the contact
    B.   a tendency to breed contempt
    C.   greater understanding and acceptance
    D.   of little importance one way or the other

5. Negativism is MOST typical of children at the age of _______ year(s).   5.____

    A.   one   B.   three   C.   six   D.   nine

6. Children's groups about the age of two typically show   6.____

    A.   much cooperation   B.   sex segregation
    C.   parallel activity   D.   none of the above

7. In which of the following functions does development depend MOST completely upon maturation?   7.____

    A.   Roller skating   B.   Swimming
    C.   Singing   D.   Walking

8. In the first months of an infant's life, the baby's reflex responses are   8.____

    A.   almost the only reactions the baby shows
    B.   virtually absent from behavior
    C.   more accurate than later in life
    D.   less conspicuous than generalized mass reactions

9. Play and reading interests of boys and girls will be found to be most DIFFERENT at the age of _______ years.

   A. three　　　　B. six　　　　C. twelve　　　　D. eighteen

10. The unsociability often reported for very bright children is MOST likely to be due to

    A. their biological makeup
    B. their complete absorption in intellectual pursuits
    C. their lack of personal attractiveness
    D. the absence of suitable companions

11. If we measure a number of individuals upon a variety of complex mental functions, we will find that the different functions show _______ relationship.

    A. a negative
    B. no
    C. a fairly high degree of positive
    D. practically a perfect positive

12. Of the following general statements about deterioration in mental patients, which is the MOST questionable at present?

    A. More recently acquired forms of reaction are lost before those formed earlier in life.
    B. Generalization and abstraction in psychoses is qualitatively the same as that in the young child.
    C. Deterioration in many cases regarded as hopeless appears to be reversible.
    D. The responses of a deteriorated person show generally a definite patterning which tends to mask his defects.

13. Concerning the course of intellectual deterioration in the mental disorders, it is CORRECT to state that

    A. defect in the ability to generalize is more characteristic of schizophrenia than of other psychotic states
    B. concept formation deteriorates more slowly in schizophrenia than in senile psychosis
    C. decreased speed and persistence in mental activity are characteristic of epilepsy
    D. senile patients suffer more impairment in the recall of long past events than in recent memory

14. According to mental test comparisons of cooperative patients in the various disease groups, the group which shows the LEAST intellectual impairment is

    A. paranoid schizophrenia　　　　B. psychopathic personality
    C. hebephrenic schizophrenia　　　D. hysteria

15. Schizophrenic speech is BEST characterized by

    A. loose, approximate use of words and reaction to superficial similarities among ideas and objects
    B. loose, approximate use of words and failure to make use of similarities or analogies

    C.   unusual amount of stammering and reaction to superficial similarities among ideas and objects
    D.   unusual amount of stammering and failure to make use of similarities or analogies

16. It is the central, distinguishing feature of the depressive phase of manic-depressive psychosis that the patient   16.____

    A.   is keenly aware of lacking a motive for existence
    B.   attaches his depression to some irrelevant or imaginary cause
    C.   is excessively disturbed over some recent trouble
    D.   is overactive, restless, and even agitated

17. In which of the following abilities do dull and gifted children tend to differ most markedly?   17.____

    A.   Arithmetical computation
    B.   Drawing
    C.   Reading comprehension
    D.   Spelling

18. The schizophrenic patient is said to exhibit loss of affect. This amounts to   18.____

    A.   decreased attention to one's personal feeling tone
    B.   lack of emotional reaction toward abstract ideas
    C.   increased affectivity to ideas and decreased affectivity concerning persons and events
    D.   increased affectiveness in environment but less to abstractions

19. Ability to establish a conditioned response in the eyelid has been found to be a point of differentiation between   19.____

    A.   idiopathic epilepsy and hysterical seizures
    B.   malingering and traumatic neurosis
    C.   senile dementia and cerebral arteriosclerosis
    D.   hysterical and organic blindness

20. The MAIN distinction between normal grief and reactive neurosis is in the   20.____

    A.   feelings of inadequacy and unreality
    B.   lack of basis in real occurrence
    C.   duration and intensity of the emotional display
    D.   intellectual retardation

21. Kretschmer's dysplastic type applies to those with   21.____

    A.   compact, round, fleshy habitus
    B.   strong, solid, muscular build
    C.   slender bodies, long bones, little muscular strength
    D.   conspicuous disharmony due to abnormal functioning of the endocrine glands

22. Which of the following is NOT characteristic of anxiety neurosis?   22.____

    A. Increase of irritable tension
    B. Vague somatic complaints
    C. Hypersensitivity to external stimuli
    D. Temporary muscular paralysis of the limbs

23. Involutional melancholia is usually characterized by a   23.____

    A. marked motor agitation   B. motor depression
    C. flight of ideas   D. loss of affect

24. From our knowledge about hallucinatory phenomena, it can be stated reliably that   24.____

    A. hallucinations occur in association with a dreamlike state
    B. hallucinations and imagery are similar processes differing only in intensity
    C. mescal-induced hallucinations are not similar to schizophrenic hallucinations
    D. organized hallucinations can be produced by direct stimulation of the brain surface

25. Which of the following is NOT a form of epilepsy?   25.____

    A. Grand mal   B. Pyknolepsy
    C. Jacksonian   D. Parkinsonian

KEY (CORRECT ANSWERS)

1.	B	11.	C
2.	B	12.	B
3.	D	13.	A
4.	A	14.	A
5.	B	15.	A
6.	C	16.	A
7.	D	17.	C
8.	D	18.	C
9.	C	19.	D
10.	D	20.	C

21.	D
22.	D
23.	A
24.	D
25.	D

EXAMINATION SECTION
TEST 1

DIRECTIONS: Each question or incomplete statement is followed by several suggested answers or completions. Select the one that BEST answers the question or completes the statement. *PRINT THE LETTER OF THE CORRECT ANSWER IN THE SPACE AT THE RIGHT.*

Questions 1-8.

DIRECTIONS: Questions 1 through 8 are to be answered on the basis of the following statement.

The child lives in a context which is itself neither simple nor unitary and which continuously affects his behavior and development. Patterns of stimulation come to him out of this context. In turn, by virtue of his own make-up, he selects from that context. At all times, there is a reciprocal relation between the human organism and this biosocial context. Because the child is limited in time, behavior becomes structured, and patterns develop both in the stimulus field and in his own response system. Some stimulus patterns become significant because they modify the developmental stream by affecting practice or social relations with others. Others remain insignificant because they do not affect this web of relations. Why one pattern is significant and another is not is a crucial problem for child psychology.

1. The author states that

    A. environmental forces have an important effect in determining both the child's actions and his course of growth
    B. environmental and hereditary forces play an equal part in determining both the child's actions and his course of growth
    C. even the environmental forces which are not consciously important to the child can affect both learning and personality
    D. the child's personality is shaped more by the total pattern of pressures in the environment

1.____

2. The author develops *context* so as to make it mean

    A. the nature of the child's immediate environment
    B. a complex rather than a simple home structure
    C. a multitude of past, present, and future forces
    D. internal as well as external influences

2.____

3. According to the author, the CRITICAL forces to be studied are those which

    A. are unconscious forces
    B. are conscious, unconscious, and subconscious forces
    C. cause the child to respond
    D. modify the child's interpersonal relationships

3.____

4. The author's point of view might BEST be labeled as 4.____

    A. environmentalist   B. behaviorist
    C. psychobiosocial   D. gestaltist

5. The author maintains that the environment 5.____

    A. is relatively stable
    B. is in a constant state of flux
    C. shows periods of marked instability
    D. is more stable than unstable

6. From the above paragraph, it is to be inferred that the 6.____

    A. child's personality is mechanistically determined by the nature of the environment
    B. unique interaction between the child and his environment shapes his personality
    C. child really shapes his own personality
    D. child's personality is more likely to be affected by than to affect the environment

7. By *structured behavior,* the author means 7.____

    A. conditioning of responses
    B. differentiated activity
    C. characteristic modes of reaction
    D. responses that have been modified by the developmental stream

8. The *patterns* to which the author refers are 8.____

    A. different for all children
    B. culturally determined mainly
    C. biologically determined mainly
    D. psychologically determined mainly

Questions 9-13.

DIRECTIONS: Questions 9 through 13 are to be answered on the basis of the following passage.

    The Division of Child Guidance makes certain provisions for summer vacations for children receiving foster care. Foster parents wishing to take the child on a vacation within the United States must file Form CG-42 in duplicate at the office of the Division not later than 3 weeks prior to the starting date of the planned vacation. Such request must be approved in writing by the Social Investigator and the Assistant Supervisor. After the request has been approved, the original copy of Form CG-42 must be returned to the foster parents by the Social Investigator no later than 3 days prior to the planned starting date of the vacation. The city continues to pay the foster parents the standard rate for the child's care.

    If the foster parents plan to take the child on a vacation outside the continental United States, Form CG-42 must be submitted in triplicate and must be received no later than 5 weeks prior to the starting date of the planned vacation. Such Form CG-42 for vacation outside the country must also be approved by the Case Supervisor. There will be no payment for time spent outside the United States.

When the approved original Form CG-42 is returned to the foster parents, it shall be accompanied by an original copy of Form CG-43. A duplicate copy of Form CG-43 shall be forwarded by the Case Supervisor to the Children's Accounts Section to stop payment for time expected to be spent outside the United States.

9. When a foster parent plans to take his foster child on a vacation trip, the Division of Child Guidance must receive Form 9.____

    A. CG-42 in triplicate no later than five weeks prior to the scheduled start of his vacation trip to Canada
    B. CG-42 in duplicate no later than three weeks prior to the scheduled start of his vacation trip to Mexico
    C. CG-43 in triplicate no later than three weeks prior to the scheduled start of his vacation trip to Arizona
    D. CG-43 in duplicate no later than five weeks prior to the scheduled start of his vacation trip regardless of location

10. The one of the following steps which is required in processing a request from a foster parent to take a child on a vacation trip is that the 10.____

    A. Case Supervisor send the original copy of Form CG-42 to the appropriate section in the case of a child who will spend all his vacation in a foreign country
    B. Children's Accounts Section receive the duplicate copy of Form CG-43 in the case of a child who will spend any part of his vacation in a foreign country
    C. Division of Child Guidance keep a permanent file of original copies of Form CG-43 to keep a control of all current vacation requests
    D. foster parents receive the triplicate copy of Form CG-42 from the Social Investigator in the case of a child who will spend part of his vacation in the United States

11. When a foster child spends an approved vacation with his foster father, payment for the child's care will be given to the foster father for 11.____

    A. none of the time if part of the vacation is spent in a foreign country
    B. that part of the vacation spent inside the United States but a reduced daily rate
    C. the entire period at a standard rate if the vacation is spent wholly in the United States
    D. the entire time regardless of whether or not it is spent in a foreign country

12. The Division of Child Guidance must notify a foster parent that his request to take his foster child on a vacation outside the country has been approved by sending him the approved _______ copy of Form CG-42 and _______ copy of Form CG-43. 12.____

    A. duplicate; duplicate   B. duplicate; original
    C. original; duplicate   D. original; original

13. On the basis of the above passage, children receiving foster care may be taken on a vacation trip by their foster parents to a location 13.____

    A. anywhere in the world with the written approval of the Social Investigator only
    B. of the foster parents' choosing but only with the written approval of both the Assistant Supervisor and Case Supervisor
    C. outside the United States but only with the written approval of the Social Investigator, Assistant Supervisor, and Case Supervisor
    D. within the United States with the written approval of the Case Supervisor only

Questions 14-18.

DIRECTIONS: Questions 14 through 18 are statements based on the following paragraphs. For each question, there are two statements.

Based on the information in the paragraphs, mark your answer A, B, or C, as follows:
A, if only statement 1 is correct;
B, if only statement 2 is correct;
C, if both statements are correct.
Mark your answer D if the excerpts do not contain sufficient evidence for concluding whether either or both statements are correct.

Almost 49,000 children were living in foster family homes or voluntary institutions in the state at the end of 2003. These were children whose parents or relatives were unable or unwilling to care for them in their own homes. The State Department of Social Services supervised the care of these children served under the auspices of 64 social services districts and more than 150 private agencies and institutions. Almost 8 out of every 1,000 children 18 years of age or younger were in care away from their homes at the end of 2003. This estimate does not include a substantial, but unknown, number of children living outside their own homes who were placed there by their parents, relatives, or others without the assistance of a social agency.

The number of children in care (dependent, neglected, and delinquent combined) was up by 4,500 or 10 percent over the 2000-2003 period. Both the city and state reported similar increases. In the comparable period, the state's child population (18 years or less) rose only three percent. Thus, the foster care rate showed a moderate increase to 7.7 per thousand in 2003 from 7.2 thousand in 2000. The city's foster care rate in 2003, at 10.5 per thousand, was almost twice that for upstate New York, 5.7 per thousand. (Excluding delinquent children from the total in care in the state reduces the foster care rate per thousand to 7.2 in 2003 and the comparable 2000 figure to 6.7.)

Dependent and neglected children made up about 95 percent of the total number in foster family homes and voluntary institutions in the state at the end of 2003, as they did in 2000. Delinquent children sent into care (outside the state training school system) by the Family Court accounted for only 5 percent of the total. The number of delinquent children in care rose 5 percent, as an increase in the state, 28 percent, more than offset a 13 percent decline in the city. Delinquents comprised 4.9 percent of the total number of children in care upstate at the end of 2003 and 3.9 percent in the city.

14.   1. There were 45,000 children in care away from their own homes over the 2000-2003 period.
    2. The percentage decline of delinquent children in care in the city in 2003 was offset by a greater increase in the rest of the state.

15.   1. The increase in delinquent care rate in the state from 2000 to 2003 cannot be determined from the data given.
    2. The state's foster care rate in 2003, exclusive of the city, was about one-half the rate for the city.

16.   1. In 2000 and in 2003, the percentage of dependent and neglected children in foster family homes and voluntary institutions in the state was about the same.
    2. In 2000, the number of dependent and neglected children in foster family homes and voluntary institutions in the state was 43,250.   16._____

17.   1. The city's child population rose approximately three percent from 2000 to 2003.
    2. At the end of 2003, less than 1% of the children 18 years of age or younger were in care.   17._____

18.   1. Delinquents in the city comprised 4.4 percent of the total number of children in care in the city at the end of 2000.
    2. An unsubstantial number of children living outside their own homes were placed by their parents or relatives without the assistance of a social agency.   18._____

Questions 19-25.

DIRECTIONS: Questions 19 through 25 are to be answered SOLELY on the basis of the information contained in the following paragraph. Each question consists of a statement. You are to indicate whether the statement is TRUE (T) or FALSE (F).

<u>RESPONSIBILITY OF PARENTS</u>

In a recent survey, ninety percent of the people interviewed felt that parents should be held responsible for the delinquency of their children. Forty-eight out of fifty states have laws holding parents criminally responsible for contributing to the delinquency of their children. It is generally accepted that parents are a major influence in the early moral development of their children. Yet, in spite of all this evidence, practical experience seems to prove that *punish the parents* laws are wrong. Legally, there is some question about the constitutionality of such laws. How far can one person be held responsible for the actions of another? Further, although there are many such laws, the fact remains that they are rarely used and where they are used, they fail in most cases to accomplish the end for which they were intended.

19. Nine out of ten of those interviewed held that parents should be responsible for the delinquency of their children.   19._____

20. Forty-eight percent of the states have laws holding parents responsible for contributing to the delinquency of their children.   20._____

21. Most people feel that parents have little influence on the early moral development of their children.   21._____

22. Experience seems to indicate that laws holding parents responsible for children's delinquency are wrong.   22._____

23. There is no doubt that laws holding parents responsible for delinquency of their children are within the Constitution.   23._____

24. Laws holding parents responsible for delinquent children are not often enforced.   24._____

25. *Punish the parent* laws usually achieve their purpose.   25._____

KEY (CORRECT ANSWERS)

1.	A		11.	C
2.	D		12.	D
3.	D		13.	C
4.	C		14.	B
5.	B		15.	B
6.	B		16.	A
7.	C		17.	D
8.	A		18.	D
9.	A		19.	T
10.	B		20.	F

21.	F
22.	T
23.	F
24.	T
25.	F

TEST 2

DIRECTIONS: Each question or incomplete statement is followed by several suggested answers or completions. Select the one that BEST answers the question or completes the statement. *PRINT THE LETTER OF THE CORRECT ANSWER IN THE SPACE AT THE RIGHT.*

Questions 1-3.

DIRECTIONS: Questions 1 through 3 are to be answered SOLELY on the basis of the following passage.

Undoubtedly, the ultimate solution to the housing problem of the hard-core slum does not lie in code enforcement, however defined. The only solution to that problem is demolition, clearance, and new construction. However, it is also clear that, even with government assistance, new construction is not keeping pace with the obsolescence and deterioration of the existing housing inventory of our cities. Add to this the facts of an increasing population and the continuing migration into metropolitan areas, as well as the demands for more and better housing that grow out of continuing economic prosperity and high employment, and some intimation may be gained of the dimensions of the problem of maintaining our housing supply so that it may begin to meet the need.

1. The one of the following that would be the MOST appropriate title for the above passage is   1.____

    A. PROBLEMS ASSOCIATED WITH MAINTAINING AN ADEQUATE HOUSING SUPPLY
    B. DEMOLITION AS A REMEDY FOR HOUSING PROBLEMS
    C. GOVERNMENT'S ESSENTIAL ROLE IN CODE ENFORCEMENT
    D. THE ULTIMATE SOLUTION TO THE HARD-CORE SLUM PROBLEM

2. According to the above passage, housing code enforcement is   2.____

    A. a way to encourage local initiative in urban renewal
    B. a valuable tool that has fallen into disuse
    C. inadequate as a solution to slum housing problems
    D. responsible for some of the housing problems since the code has not been adequately defined

3. The above passage makes it clear that the BASIC solution to the housing problem is to   3.____

    A. erect new buildings after demolition and site clearance
    B. discourage migration into the metropolitan area
    C. increase rents paid to landlords
    D. enforce the housing code strictly

Questions 4-5.

DIRECTIONS: Questions 4 and 5 are to be answered SOLELY on the basis of the following passage.

Under common law, the tenant was obliged to continue to pay rent, at the risk of eviction, regardless of the condition of the premises. This obligation was based on the following established common law principles: first, that in the absence of express agreement, a lease does not contain any implied warranty of fitness or habitability; second, that the person in possession of premises has the obligation to repair and maintain them; and third, that a lease conveys an interest in real estate rather than binding one to a mutual obligation. Once having conveyed his property, the landlord's right to rent was unconditional. Thus, even if he made an express agreement to repair, the landlord's right to rent remained independent of his promise to repair. This doctrine, known as the *independence of covenants,* required the tenant to continue to pay rent or risk eviction, and to bring a separate action against the landlord for damages resulting from his breach of agreement to repair.

4. According to the above passage, common law provided that a lease would   4.____

    A. bar an ex parte action
    B. bind the parties thereto to a reciprocal obligation
    C. provide an absolute defense for breach of agreement
    D. transmit an interest in real property

5. According to the above passage, the *independence of covenants* required that the   5.____

    A. tenant continue to pay rent even for unfit housing
    B. landlord hold rents in escrow for aggrieved tenants
    C. landlord show valid cause for non-performance of lease requirements
    D. tenant surrender the demised premises in improved condition

Questions 6-11.

DIRECTIONS: Questions 6 through 11 are to be answered SOLELY on the basis of the information given in the following passage.

The City of X has set up a Maximum Base Rent Program for all rent-controlled apartments. The objective is to insure that the landlord will get a fair, but not excessive, profit on his building to stem the great tide of buildings being abandoned by their owners, and to encourage landlords to continue the upkeep of their property. The Maximum Base Rent Program permits the landlord to raise rents under carefully devised standards, while practically no raises in rents in this City were permitted under previous guidelines.

Under this plan, the City determines a Maximum Base Rent amount by means of a formula which takes into account the age of the building, the number of apartments, total rents received from the building, the amount of expenses, and labor costs. The Maximum Base Rent amount is to be recomputed every two years to allow for increases or decreases in building costs.

The Maximum Base Rent, which will allow the landlord to make a *fair return* on his investment, may not be collected immediately, however, since no rent increases over 7.5 percent will be permitted in any one year. The highest actual rent for each apartment during a given year will be called the Maximum Collectible Rent. This will be computed so that the increase over the present rent is not more than 7.5 percent ($7.50 on every $100.00). Sometimes, it may be less. Therefore, collectible rents will increase each year until the Maximum Base Rent is reached.

Questions 14-18.

DIRECTIONS: Questions 14 through 18 are statements based on the following paragraphs. For each question, there are two statements.

Based on the information in the paragraphs, mark your answer A, B, or C, as follows:
A, if only statement 1 is correct;
B, if only statement 2 is correct;
C, if both statements are correct.
Mark your answer D if the excerpts do not contain sufficient evidence for concluding whether either or both statements are correct.

Almost 49,000 children were living in foster family homes or voluntary institutions in the state at the end of 2003. These were children whose parents or relatives were unable or unwilling to care for them in their own homes. The State Department of Social Services supervised the care of these children served under the auspices of 64 social services districts and more than 150 private agencies and institutions. Almost 8 out of every 1,000 children 18 years of age or younger were in care away from their homes at the end of 2003. This estimate does not include a substantial, but unknown, number of children living outside their own homes who were placed there by their parents, relatives, or others without the assistance of a social agency.

The number of children in care (dependent, neglected, and delinquent combined) was up by 4,500 or 10 percent over the 2000-2003 period. Both the city and state reported similar increases. In the comparable period, the state's child population (18 years or less) rose only three percent. Thus, the foster care rate showed a moderate increase to 7.7 per thousand in 2003 from 7.2 thousand in 2000. The city's foster care rate in 2003, at 10.5 per thousand, was almost twice that for upstate New York, 5.7 per thousand. (Excluding delinquent children from the total in care in the state reduces the foster care rate per thousand to 7.2 in 2003 and the comparable 2000 figure to 6.7.)

Dependent and neglected children made up about 95 percent of the total number in foster family homes and voluntary institutions in the state at the end of 2003, as they did in 2000. Delinquent children sent into care (outside the state training school system) by the Family Court accounted for only 5 percent of the total. The number of delinquent children in care rose 5 percent, as an increase in the state, 28 percent, more than offset a 13 percent decline in the city. Delinquents comprised 4.9 percent of the total number of children in care upstate at the end of 2003 and 3.9 percent in the city.

14.   1. There were 45,000 children in care away from their own homes over the 2000-2003 period.   14.____
      2. The percentage decline of delinquent children in care in the city in 2003 was offset by a greater increase in the rest of the state.

15.   1. The increase in delinquent care rate in the state from 2000 to 2003 cannot be determined from the data given.   15.____
      2. The state's foster care rate in 2003, exclusive of the city, was about one-half the rate for the city.

month following the date on which the apartment was vacated. He shall also prepare a reduction in Rent Roll (Form 105.046), the original of which is to be attached to the file copy of the Project Monthly Summary for the month during which the reduction is effective. Copies are to be sent to the Finance and Audit Department, Budget Section, and to the Chief of Insurance.

12. The purpose of the above paragraph is to provide for a procedure in handling　　12.____

    A. the accounting for space occupied by offices and community centers
    B. apartments not rented as of the first of the month following the date on which the apartment was vacated
    C. vacant apartments temporarily used as office space
    D. vacant apartments permanently removed from the rent roll

13. The Rent Control Book is a control on the amount of monthly rents charged.　　13.____
According to the above paragraph, another function of the Rent Control Book is to indicate the

    A. number of offices and community spaces available in the project
    B. number of dwelling units in the project
    C. number of vacant apartments in the project
    D. rental loss for all offices and community spaces

14. In accordance with the above paragraph, the original of the Form 105.046 is to be　　14.____

    A. sent to Central Office with the Project Monthly Summary
    B. kept in the project files with the project copy of the Project Monthly Summary
    C. sent to the Finance and Audit Department
    D. sent to the Chief of Insurance

15. The MOST likely reason for informing the Chief of Insurance of the removal of an apartment from the rent roll is to notify him　　15.____

    A. to make adjustments in the insurance coverage
    B. of a future change in the address of the office or community space
    C. of a change in the project rent income
    D. of a possible increase in the number of project employees

Questions 16-20.

DIRECTIONS: Questions 16 through 20 are to be answered SOLELY on the basis of the information provided in the following passage.

It is the Housing Administration's policy that all tenants, whether new or transferring from one housing development to another, should be required to pay a standard security deposit of one month's rent based on the rent at the time of admission. There are, however, certain exceptions to this policy. Employees of the Administration shall not be required to pay a security deposit if they secure an apartment in an Administration development. Where the payment of a full security deposit may present a hardship to a tenant, the development's manager may allow a tenant to move into an apartment upon payment of only part of the security deposit. In such cases, however, the tenant must agree to gradually pay the balance of the deposit. If a tenant transfers from one apartment to another within the same project, the security deposit originally paid by the tenant for his former apartment will be acceptable for his new apartment, even if the rent in the new apartment is greater than the rent in the former one. Finally, tenants who receive public assistance need not pay a security deposit before moving into an apartment if the appropriate agency states, in writing, that it will pay the deposit. However, it is the responsibility of the development's manager to make certain that payment shall be received within one month of the date that the tenant moves into the apartment.

16. According to the above passage, when a tenant transfers from one apartment to another in the same development, the Housing Administration will

    A. accept the tenant's old security deposit as the security deposit for his new apartment regardless of the new apartment's rent
    B. refund the tenant's old security deposit and not require him to pay a new deposit
    C. keep the tenant's old security deposit and require him to pay a new deposit
    D. require the tenant to pay a new security deposit based on the difference between his old rent and his new rent

17. On the basis of the above passage, it is INCORRECT to state that a tenant who receives public assistance may move into an Administration development if

    A. he pays the appropriate security deposit
    B. the appropriate agency gives a written indication that it will pay the security deposit before the tenant moves in
    C. the appropriate agency states, by telephone, that it will pay the security deposit
    D. the appropriate agency writes the manager to indicate that the security deposit will be paid within one month but not less than two weeks from the date the tenant moves into the apartment

18. On the basis of the above passage, a tenant who transfers from an apartment in one development to an apartment in a different development will

    A. forfeit his old security deposit and be required to pay another deposit
    B. have his old security deposit refunded and not have to pay a new deposit
    C. pay the difference between his old security deposit and the new one
    D. have to pay a security deposit based on the new apartment's rent

19. The Housing Administration will NOT require payment of a security deposit if a tenant

    A. is an Administration employee
    B. is receiving public assistance
    C. claims that payment will present a hardship
    D. indicates, in writing, that he will be responsible for any damage done to his apartment

20. Of the following, the BEST title for the above passage is

    A. SECURITY DEPOSITS - TRANSFERS
    B. SECURITY DEPOSITS - POLICY
    C. EXEMPTIONS AND EXCEPTIONS - SECURITY DEPOSITS
    D. AMOUNTS - SECURITY DEPOSITS

Questions 21-23.

DIRECTIONS: Questions 21 through 23 are to be answered SOLELY on the basis of the following paragraphs.

In our program, we must continually strive to increase public good will and to maintain that good will which we have already established. It is important to remember in all your public contacts that to a good many people you are the Department. Don't take out any of your personal gripes on the public. When we must appeal to the public for cooperation, that is when any good will we have built up will come in handy. If the public has been given incorrect or incomplete help when seeking information or advice, or have received what they considered poor treatment in dealing with members of the Department, they will not provide a sympathetic audience when we direct our appeals to them.

One of the Department activities in which there is considerable contact with the public is inspection. Any activity in this area poses special problems and makes your personal dealings with the individuals involved very important. You must bear in mind that you are dealing with people who are sensitive to the manner in which they are treated and you should guide yourself accordingly.

Let us consider some of the aspects of the actual inspection of the premises:

APPEARANCE - Your appearance will determine the initial impression made on anyone you deal with. It is often difficult to change a person's first impression, so try to make it a favorable one. Be neat and clean; show that you have taken some trouble to make a good appearance. Your appearance should form a part of a business-like attitude that should govern your inspection of any premises.

APPROACH - Be courteous at all times. When you enter a building, immediately seek out the owner or occupant and ask his permission to inspect the premises. Ask him to accompany you on the inspection if he has the time, and explain to him the reasons why such inspections are made. Try to give him the feeling that this is a cooperative effort and that his part in this effort is appreciated. Do not make your approach on the basis that it is your legal right to inspect the premises; a coercive attitude tends to produce a hostile reaction.

21. Of the following, the BEST title for the subject covered in the above paragraphs is   21._____

    A. GOOD MANNERS   B. PUBLIC RELATIONS
    C. NEATNESS   D. INSPECTIONAL DUTIES

22. According to the above paragraphs, the FIRST impression an inspector makes on the   22._____
public is that of

    A. sympathy   B. courtesy
    C. cleanliness and dress   D. business attitude

23. According to the above paragraphs, if you want the public to cooperate with you, you   23._____
must

    A. be available at all times
    B. be sure that any information you give them is correct
    C. make sure that their complaints are justified
    D. be stern in your dealings with landlords

Questions 24-25.

DIRECTIONS: Questions 24 and 25 are to be answered SOLELY on the basis of the following passage.

There is no simple solution for controlling crime and deviant behavior. There is no panacea for anti-social conduct. The sooner society gives up the search for a single control solution, the sooner society will be able to face up to the immensity of the task and the never-ending responsibility of our social structure.

24. Which of the following statements is BEST supported by the above passage?　24._____

    A. Although crime causation may be considered singular, crime control is many-faceted.
    B. When society faces up to the immensity of the crime problem, it will find a single solution to it.
    C. A multi-faceted approach to crime control is better than trying to find a single cause or cure.
    D. Our social structure is responsible for a continuing search for a simple solution to anti-social behavior.

25. The crime problem can be solved when　25._____

    A. it is realized that no solution exists
    B. the problem is specifically identified
    C. criminals are punished
    D. none of the above

KEY (CORRECT ANSWERS)

1. A		11. B	
2. C		12. D	
3. A		13. B	
4. D		14. B	
5. A		15. A	
6. D		16. A	
7. B		17. C	
8. A		18. D	
9. A		19. A	
10. C		20. B	

21.	B
22.	C
23.	B
24.	C
25.	D

MATHEMATICS
EXAMINATION SECTION
TEST 1

DIRECTIONS : Each question or incomplete statement is followed by several suggested answers or completions. Select the one that *BEST* answers the question or completes the statement. *PRINT THE LETTER OF THE CORRECT ANSWER IN THE SPACE AT THE RIGHT.*

[Ability No. 1. *Determine the time between two events.*(Questions 1-4)]

1. School starts at 7:45 a.m. The last period ends at 2:10 p.m. How long is the school day?

    A. 5 hours 35 minutes
    B. 6 hours 25 minutes
    C. 6 hours 35 minutes
    D. 535 minutes

    1.____

2. You get to the bus station in Orlando at 8:30 a.m. How long do you have to wait for the next bus to Tallahassee? (See Schedule below)

    A. 1 hour 10 minutes
    B. 3 hours 15 minutes
    C. 4 hours 50 minutes
    D. 7 hours 10 minutes

    2.____

THE GRAYFOX BUS LINES, Orlando, Florida				
Arrivals			**Departures**	
From	Time		To	Time
Tampa	5:30 a.m.		Miami	7:45 a.m.
Jacksonvl	6:50 a.m.		Melbourne	9:30 a.m.
Melbourne	8:30 a.m.		Tampa	12:00 p.m.
Tallahassee	11:45 a.m.		Tallahassee	1:20 p.m.

3. Mr. Arnold parks his car at the airport to catch a plane. Entering the parking lot, he picks up a ticket which reads: 13 Nov 3:20 p.m. He checks his car out on November 15 at 8:30 a.m.
   How long was his car in the parking lot?

    A. 1 day, 5 hours,10 minutes
    B. 1 day, 17 hours, 1O minutes
    C. 2 days, 4 hours, 50 minutes
    D. 2 days, 5 hours,10 minutes

    3.____

4. The Army had a special 30-month recruitment program. Pete joined the Army on October 1, 2010.
   When will Pete be discharged?

    A. May 1, 2012
    B. March 1, 2013
    C. April 1, 2013
    D. May 1, 2013

    4.____

[Ability No. 2. *Determine equivalent amounts of money.* (Questions 5-8)]

5. Look at the picture at the top of the next page. How much money do you have?

    A. $28.97   B. $29.27   C. $29.52   D. $29.77

    5.____

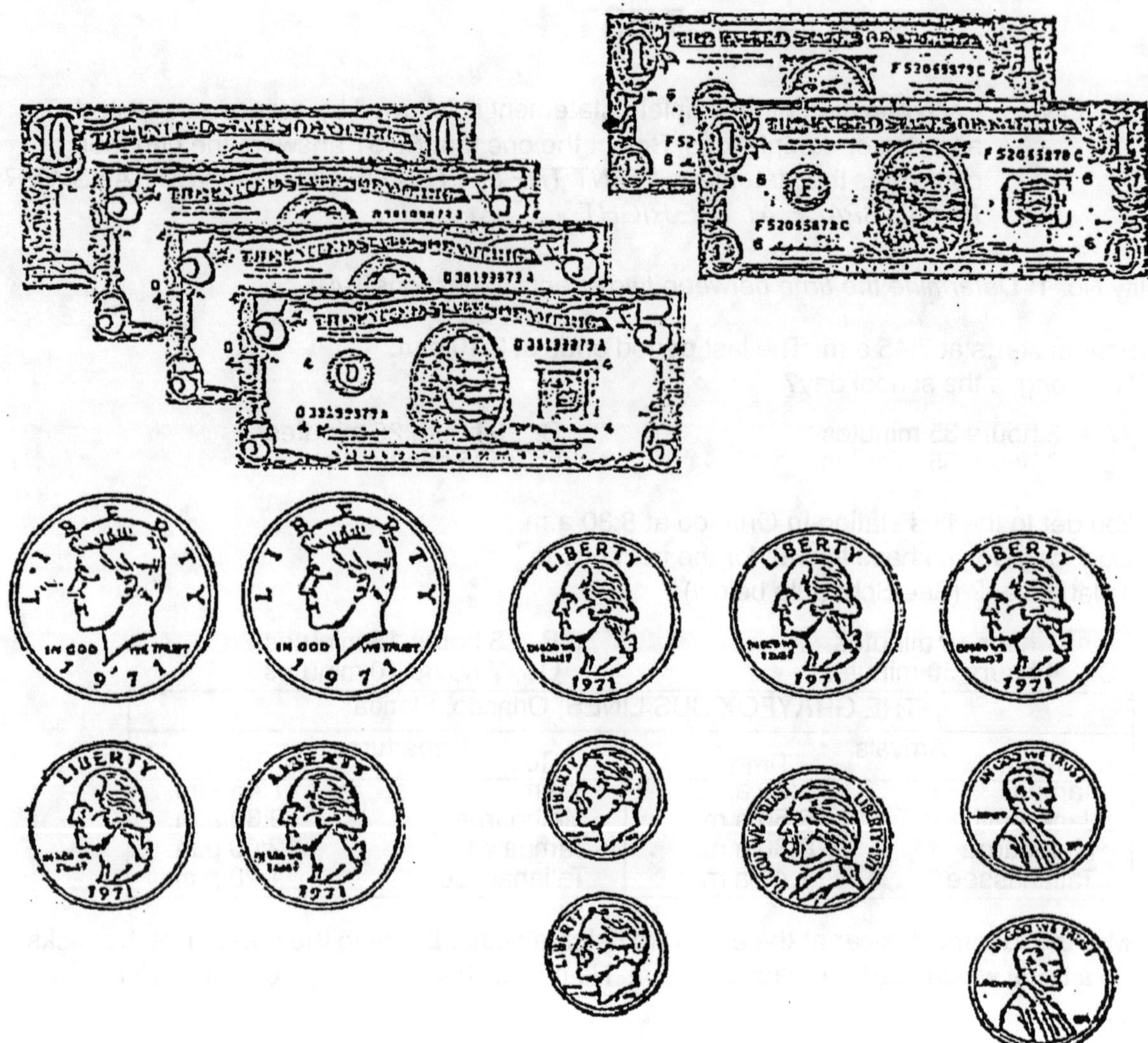

6. You are a cashier in a cafeteria. A customer's bill comes to $3.48, with tax. He gives you   6._____
   a $10 bill. Which of the following would be his change?

   A. Seven dollars - four dimes - one nickel - three pennies
   B. Seven dollars - two quarters - two pennies
   C. Six dollars - two quarters - two pennies
   D. Six dollars - four dimes - one nickel - three pennies

7. A book costs $7.58. You pay for the book with a $20 bill. The cashier counts your change   7._____
   as follows:"60 cents, 65 cents, 75 cents, 8 dollars, 9 dollars, 10 dollars, 15 dollars, 20 dollars."
   Which of the following shows the coins and bills you *most likely* received?

   A. 2 pennies, 1 nickel, 1 dime, 1 quarter, 3 dollar bills, 1 five-dollar bill
   B. 2 pennies, 1 nickel, 1 dime, 1 quarter, 3 dollar bills, 2 five-dollar bills
   C. 2 pennies, 1 nickel, 1 dime, 1 quarter, 2 dollar bills, 2 five-dollar bills
   D. 3 pennies, 1 nickel, 1 dime, 1 quarter, 2 dollar bills, 2 five-dollar bills

8. You are a clerk in a store. A customer's purchases come to $28.73. He gives you two twenty-dollar bills.
   Which of the following would be the *correct* change?

8.____

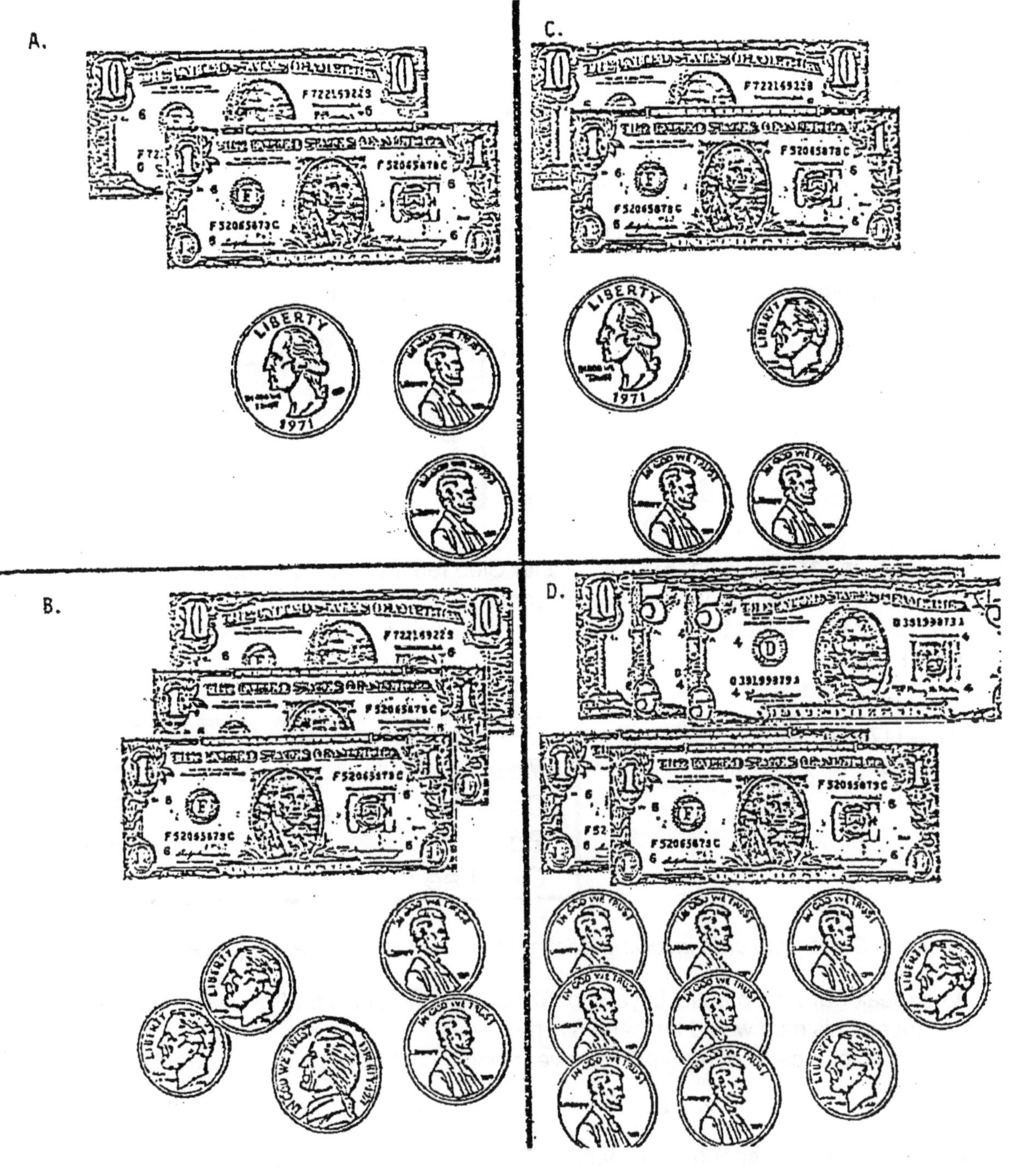

[Ability No. 3. *Solve problems involving whole numbers.* (Questions 9-13)]

9. Mr. Johnson maps out a route from Miami to Pensacola, The distance is 685 miles. If Mr. Johnson drives this distance in about 14 hours, his *average* driving speed was about how many miles per hour?

9.____

   A. 40   B. 45   C. 50   D. 55

10. The High and Mighty High School is a two-story building. There are 16 classrooms on each floor. One period there were exactly 25 students in each room.
How many students were in class that period?

   A. 224   B. 400   C. 790   D. 800

10.____

11. A swimming pool holds 30,000 gallons of water.
If water is pumped out of the pool at the rate of 50 gallons per minute, how long will it take to drain the pool?

   A. 6 hours   B. 10 hours   C. 60 hours   D. 600 hours

11.____

12. Chuck is in charge of buying the chicken for the class picnic. He buys 3 buckets, 5 barrels, and 1 tub.
How many pieces of chicken did he get? (See Menu at right)

   A. 84
   B. 111
   C. 186
   D. 198

12.____

Menu	
Size	No. Pieces
Box	5
Bucket	15
Barrel	21
Tub	48

13. The High and Mighty High. School Booster Club rented 1 van, 2 coaches, and 1 bus to take students to an out-of-town football game.
In order for the project to be a sell-out, how many tickets must the club sell? (See table below)

   A. 97
   B. 117
   C. 127
   D. 187

13.____

Seating Capacity	
Van	12
Coach	30
Bus	55
Cruiser	90

[Ability No. 4. *Solve problems involving decimal numbers and percents. (Questions 14-17)*]

14. A car dealer urged potential buyers to take advantage of his end-of-year sale, because the price of his cars would increase 8% next year.
For example, a car costing $6200 this year would cost how much next year?

   A. $496   B. $4960   C. $6208   D. $6696

14.____

15. A family decided to spend their vacation visiting New York state parks. They drove 1436 miles and used 62.4 gallons of gasoline.
On this trip, they got how many miles per gallon?

   A. 23.0   B. 23.1   C. 23.8   D. 89,606

15.____

16. The Simpson family was planning a big reunion. Mrs. Simpson bought two turkeys, one   16._____
    weighing 14.5 pounds and one weighing 23.0 pounds.
    How much did she pay for the turkeys?

    A. $13.57
    B. $22.13
    C. $23.58
    D. $221.25

Turkey Sale	
Weight	Cost/lb.
8-11 lbs.	79¢
12-18 lbs.	69¢
19-25 lbs.	59¢

17. A label on a pair of pants warns that 8% shrinkage may be expected after washing.   17._____
    If the length of the new pants is 30 inches, after washing the length may be only

    A. 24 inches   B. 27.6 inches
    C. 29.76 inches   D. 32.4 inches

[Ability No. 5. *Solve problems involving comparison shopping.* (Questions 18-22)]

18. The ad says that you can buy an air gun for $29.90 cash plus $1.87 for postage and han-   18._____
    dling. Or, you may make 6 equal payments of $5.41.
    How much do you save by paying for the gun in a *SINGLE* payment?

    A. $0.00   B. $0.60   C. $0.87   D. $1.87

19. Super-Gen radial tires are on sale. Four stores advertise their terms for the sale of the   19._____
    same tire. If you are buying four tires, which store offers the *BEST* price?

A. 

B. 

C. 

D. 

20. You receive the following advertisement for a satellite radio in the mail.
How much more do you pay if you decide to pay for the radio in six installments?

20.____

A. nothing
B. $0.01
C. $1.98
D. $40.01

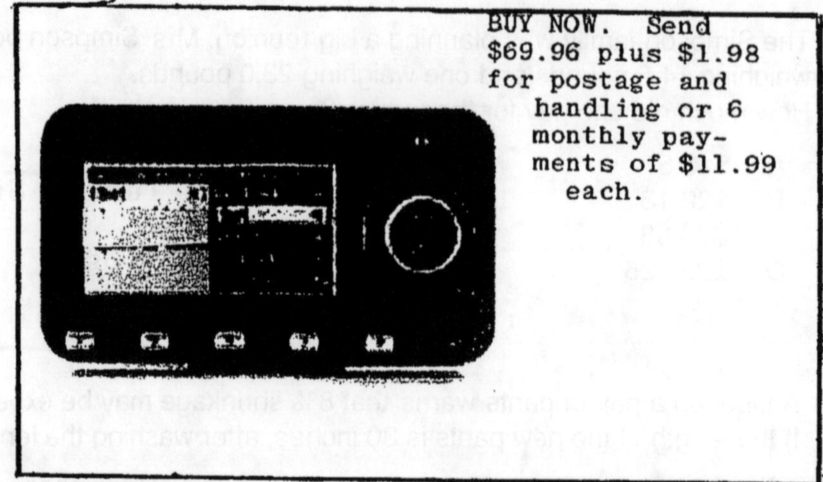

21. Spotless Miracle detergent is packaged in boxes of four different sizes: regular, large, giant, commercial.
Which size of container is the *BEST* buy per ounce?

21.____

A. Regular
B. Large
C. Giant
D. Commercial

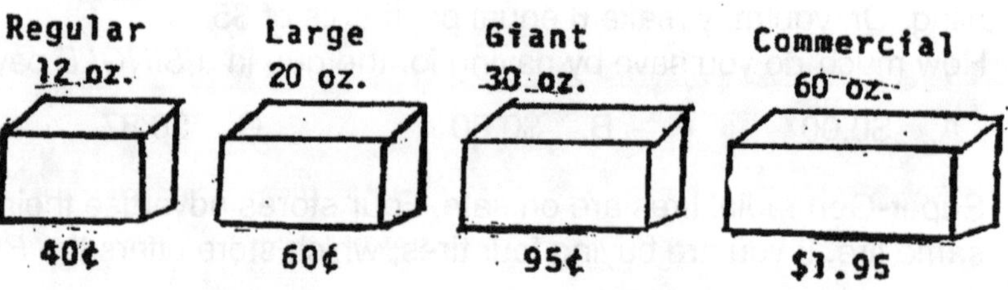

22. A package of 8 hamburger buns costs 65¢. A package of 12 buns costs 95¢. You need to buy 4 dozen buns.
What would you *save* If you bought packages of 12 instead of packages of 8?

22.____

A. $0.10
B. $0.30
C. Nothing.   The cost is the same.
D. Nothing.   You would lose money.

[Ability No. 6. *Solve problems involving a rate of interest.* (Questions 23-27)]

23. A savings bank runs the following ad (see figure) of a new savings plan.
If you invest $800, how much money will you have in the account at the end of one year?

23.____

A. $40
B. $64
C. $840
D. $864

A NEW IDEA in savings.
A savings plan paying
8% per annum.
Minimum investment: $500

24. A college loan fund provides money for educational expenses. The terms of loan are as follows: No interest is charged on money borrowed while the student is in school. After the student leaves school, interest at the rate of 5% per year is charged on the total amount borrowed.
If a student had borrowed $3800 from the fund, how much interest will he owe one year after graduation?

24.____

A. $150   B. $190   C. $3950   D. $3990

25. A bank's interest rate on regular passbook savings accounts is 6% per annum payable   25._____
    quarterly.
    If you open an account with $200, how much interest will you earn the first 3 months?

    A. $1.00   B. $3.00   C. $12.00   D. $30.00

26. You buy a car for $3000 - $500 down, balance in 36 equal payments. The finance charge   26._____
    is 10% per year on the original unpaid balance for 3 years.
    What is the amount of interest you pay?

    A. $250   B. $300   C. $500   D. $750

27. Barbara earned $1300 as a lifeguard at a summer resort. She spent $400 and put the   27._____
    remainder in a savings account. The savings plan paid interest semi-annually at the rate
    of 6% per annum.
    At the end of six months, how much was in Barbara's savings account?

    A. $54   B. $78   C. $927   D. $954

[Ability No. 7. *Solve purchase problems involving sales tax,* (Questions 28-32)]

Questions 28-32.

DIRECTIONS: Information on how to figure the State Sales Tax is provided in the table below.
              Refer to this table as you do Questions 28-32.

STATE SALES TAX	
Amount of Purchase	Tax
10¢-25¢	1¢
26¢-50¢	2¢
51¢-75¢	3¢
76¢-$1.00	4¢
$1.01 -$1.25	5¢

The tax is 4¢ on each whole dollar above $1. The tax on part of a dollar can be found from the scale above.

28. The menu price of the Fisherman's Net is $6.50. What is the cost of the dinner after add-   28._____
    ing the sales tax?

    A. 24¢   B. 26¢   C. $6.74   D. $6.76

29. The State Sales Tax is applied to motel and hotel room charges. Some cities also assess   29._____
    a 1% Resort Tax on room charges.
    If a room rents for $40 per day, what is the *TOTAL* weekly charge for this room, includ-
    ing the sales and resort taxes?

    A. $2.00   B. $42.00   C. $294.00   D. $294.11

30. You buy a power drill on sale (see ad).
How much do you pay for it, including
the sales tax?
   A. $3.12
   B. $10.28
   C. $13.51
   D. $13.52

30._____

31. The State sales tax on new cars is 4%. *the* sticker price of a car including extras, title,
transportation, and dealer preparation is $35,000.
What is the *TOTAL* cost of the car, including sales tax?

   A. $1,400   B. $35,140   C. $36,200   D. $36,400

31._____

32. A new van costs $28,500. Trader Vic is offering a $4,500 end-of-year discount on this
van. If you buy the van on sale, you will also have a savings on the sales tax you pay.
How much is the *TOTAL* savings, discount plus savings on sales tax?

   A. $180   B. $960   C. $4,680   D. $5,460

32._____

Ability No. 8. *Solve purchase problems involving discounts* (Questions 33-36)]

33. Jeans are on sale. How much would
you save on 2 pairs?
   A. $5
   B. $10
   C. $20
   D. $30

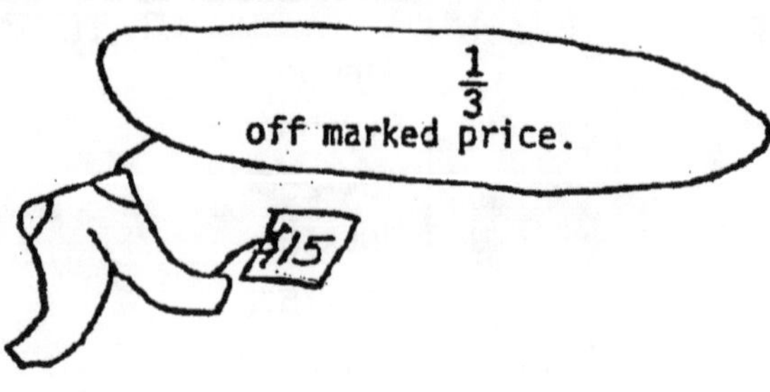

33._____

34. A sporting goods store is giving a 20% discount on all tennis equipment.
What would be the total bill, before tax, on the following items?

   A. $5.80
   B. $31.20
   C. $33.20
   D. $39.00

Tennis racket	$25
Can tennis balls. . .	$ 4
Football.	$10

34._____

35. A store is having an Anniversary Sale. For details, refer to the table below. What would
be the sale price of a sofa which regularly sells for $258?

   A. $77.40
   B. $180.60
   C. $206.40
   D. $258.00

STOREWIDE DISCOUNTS		
10% discount on purchases from $10–$100	20% discount on purchases from $101–$200	30% discount on purchases over $200

35._____

36. The following ad was run for a going-out-of-business sale.
Altogether, how much would
you have to pay for a shirt, a pair of
jeans, and a sweater?

```
        LAST CHANCE BARGAINS
Shirts    - reg. $10      1/4 off
Jeans     - reg. $15      1/3 off
Hats      - reg. $ 6      1/2 off
Sweaters  - reg. $24      1/3 off
Belts     - reg. $7.50    1/4 off
```

   A. $15.50
   B. $29.50
   C. $33.50
   D. $49.00

36.____

[Ability No, 9. *Solve problems involving measurement.* (Questions 37-40)]

Questions 37-38.

DIRECTIONS: Use this table with Problems 37 and 38.

```
12 inches  = 1 foot
  3 feet   = 1 yard
1760 yards = 1 mile
5280 feet  = 1 mile
```

37. Agnes plans to make new curtains for her living room.
She estimates that it will take 55 inches of material for each curtain panel.
About how many yards of material should she buy to make 8 of the panels?

   A. 1 1/2 yards   B. 13 yards   C. 14 yards   D. 37 yards

37.____

38. Ten (10) laps around the school track is one mile. What is the distance around the track?

   A. 176 yards   B. 528 yards
   C. 17,600 yards   D. 52,800 yards

38.____

Questions 39-40.

DIRECTIONS: Use this table with Problems 39 and 40.

```
1 centimeter = 10 millimeters
    1 meter  = 100 centimeters
1 kilometer  = 1000 meters
```

39. About how much shelf space is needed to store 4 boxes with widths of 30.4 cm?

   A. 11 meters   B. 21 meters
   C. .30 meter   D. 121.60 meters

39.____

40. Seventy-five (75) sections of pipe are laid to connect the Haningers' house to the nearest water main.
If the distance between the Haningers' house and the water main is 2.28 kilometers,
how long is each section of pipe?

   A. 3.04 meters   B. 30.4 meters   C. 34 meters   D. 684 meters

40.____

[Ability No. 9. *Solve problems involving the area of a rectangle* (Questions 41-44)]

41. A carpet-cleaning company figures the cost of cleaning carpets on a sliding scale (see table). A school has 40 yards of carpeted hallways. The halls are 3-1/3 yards wide. How much per square yard will the company charge the school to clean the hallways?

CHARGES FOR CLEANING CARPET	
Number Sq. Yards	Cost/Sq. Yard
5–50	$3.25
51–100	$3.10
101–150	$2.85
over 150	$2.50

   A. $3.25
   B. $3.10
   C. $2.85
   D. $2.50

41.____

42. A company has a 2.5-meter-high wire fence around its equipment storage area. The area measures 30 meters by 50 meters. The company plans to add extra security to the. area by stringing 3 strands of barbed wire along the top of the fence.
How many meters of barbed wire does the company need for this job?

   A. 160 meters   B. 240 meters   C. 480 meters   D. 960 meters

42.____

43. One liter of paint will cover about 50 square meters. How many liters of paint should you buy to cover a rectangular area which measures 20.1 meters by 28.9 meters?

   A. 1 liter   B. 11 liters   C. 12 liters   D. 581 liters

43.____

44. You are going to bake cookies in a 9-inch by 12-inch pan. How many cookies will you have if you cut them into 3-inch squares?

   A. 9   B. 12   C. 27   D. 36

44.____

[Ability No. 10. *Solve problems involving capacity* (Questions 45-48)]

Questions 45-46.

DIRECTIONS: Use the following table with Problems 45 and 46.

```
 3 teaspoons   = 1 tablespoon
16 tablespoons = 1 cup
    2 cups  = 1 pint
    2 pints = 1 quart
    4 quarts = 1 gallon
```

45. Adam buys a new 15-gallon aquarium. The directions say to put no more than 13.5 gallons of water in the tank. This allows an air space at the top and room for decorations and equipment. Adam doesn't have a gallon container, but he does have a quart jar. How many quarts are needed to fill the tank to the specified level?

   A. 3.375   B. 3.75   C. 54   D. 60

45.____

46. Bret is preparing an insecticide solution to spray on his fruit trees. The directions are to mix 3 tablespoons of the insecticide concentrate with each gallon of water, Bret should add how much insecticide concentrate to 20 gallons of water?

   A. 1 1/4 cups   B. 3 3/4 cups   C. 5 1/3 cups   D. 6 2/3 cups

46.____

Questions 47-48.

DIRECTIONS: Use the following table with Problems 47 and 48.

```
250 milliliters = 1 metric cup
  4 metric cups = 1 liter
1000 milliliters = 1 liter
```

47. The ratio for mixing oil and gas for a certain motor is 200 ml of outboard motor oil to 3 liters of gasoline. Using this ratio, one liter of motor oil should be mixed with what quantity of gasoline?

    A.   5 liters   B.   15 liters   C.   66 liters   D.   600 liters

47.____

48. A big economy bottle of Cheer-Up contains 2.5 liters. About *how many* 150-ml servings are there in one bottle?

    A.   6   B.   17   C.   60   D.   167

48.____

[Ability No. 11. *Solve problems involving weight* (Questions 49-52)]

Questions 49-50.

DIRECTIONS: Use the following table with Problems 49 and 50.

```
  16 ounces = 1 pound
2000 pounds = 1 ton
```

49. A farmer has a grove of 1000 fruit trees.
If he plans to use 5 pounds of fertilizer per tree, *how many* tons of fertilizer should he buy?

    A.   200 pounds   B.   2.5 tons
    C.   5 tons   D.   10,000 pounds

49.____

50. Hamburger patties for Mac's King are made by a machine. The machine is set to make 100 patties out of 20 pounds of hamburger.
Patties at this setting of the machine weigh how much?

    A.   Exactly 3 ozs.
    B.   A little more than 3 ozs.
    C.   A little less than 5 ozs.
    D.   Exactly 5 ozs.

50.____

Questions 51-52.

DIRECTIONS: Use the following table with Problems 51 and 52.

```
1000 milligrams = 1 gram
   1000 grams = 1 kilogram
1000 kilograms = 1 metric ton
```

51. A shipping label contains the following information (see figure).   51.____
   What is the *TOTAL* weight of just the boat, motor, and trailer?
   A. 1.25 metric tons
   B. 2.4 metric tons
   C. 2.5 metric tons
   D. 2.7 metric tons

Item	Weight
Boat	1350 kilograms
Motor	425 kilograms
Trailer	725 kilograms
Packing	200 kilograms

52. Chet has a 3-metric-ton truck. That is, his truck can carry a load of 3 metric tons. Chet   52.____
   has a freight order to carry 60 surfboards weighing 40 kilograms each.
   The weight of this load is how much below the load capacity of his truck?

   A. 600 kilograms
   C. 1600 kilograms
   B. 1400 kilograms
   D. 2400 kilograms

[Ability No. 12. *Find the information in graphs and tables* (Questions 53-59)]

53. This is an advertisement for a tire sale (see figure). How much does a H78-15 sized tire   53.____
   cost on sale?
   A. $39.60
   B. $40.80
   C. $46.41
   D. $75.21

TUBELESS WHITEWALL SIZE	REGULAR PRICE EACH	SALE PRICE EACH	PLUS F.E.T. EACH
A78-13	$46	27.60	2.06
C78-14	$55	33.00	2.33
E78-14	$59	35.40	2.55
F78-14	$63	37.80	2.82
G78-14	$66	39.60	2.97
H78-14	$68	40.80	3.24
G78-15	$68	40.80	3.03
H78-15	$72	43.20	3.21
J78-15†	$77	46.20	3.32
L78-15†	$50	48.00	3.46

NO TRADE-IN NEEDED. †4 ply polyester cord plies.

54. Each day the National Weather Service reports the low and high temperatures and the   54.____
   precipitation for selected cities.
   In this report, the maximum temperature in the state was reported in which city? (See
   chart)

   A. Tallahassee
   B. Jacksonville
   C. Miami
   D. Orlando

Florida Cities			
Apalachicola	87	73	.31
Crestview	91	69	...
Daytona Bch	87	71	...
Ft Lauderdale	88	77	...
Ft Myers	90	74	...
Gainesville	90	66	...
Homestead	91	68	...
Jacksonville	84	63	.33
Key West	89	79	...
Lakeland	93	73	...

Miami	89	75	. . .
Orlando	94	74	. . .
Pensacola	88	80	. . .
Sarasota	89	69	. . .
Tallahassee	83	69	1.23
Tampa	91	75	. . .
Vero Beach	90	71	. . .
Wst Plm Bch	90	71	. . .

55. A bank prepared a graph to help its customers plan their budgets (see figure). Following the bank's recommendations. if you earn $80 weekly, about how much should you spend on a car?

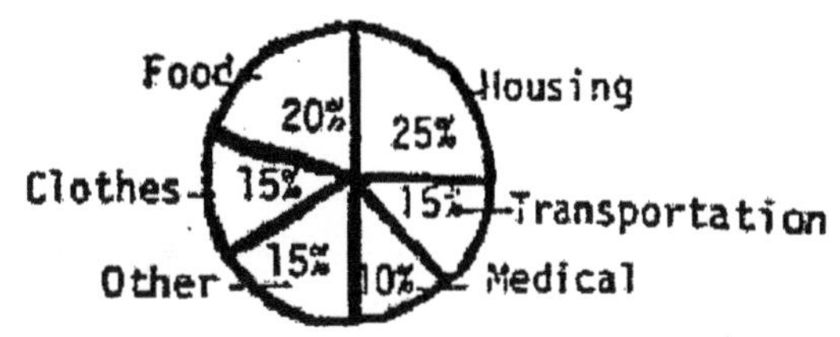

A. $8
B. $12
C. $15
D. $120

55.____

56. A consumers' group prepares reports on changes in the cost of selected items. This report shows the changes in the cost of coffee during a one-year period. According to this report, the cost of a pound of coffee rose how much from April 1 to July 1?

56.____

A. $0.50
B. $1.00
C. $1.50
D. $2.50

57. A certain type of cereal provides the following vitamins and minerals. If you ate 2 ounces of the cereal, you would have what percent of your daily need of iron?

57.____

A. 4%
B. 15%
C. 30%
D. 166%

PERCENTAGE OF U.S. RECOM- MENDED DAILY ALLOWANCES (U.S.R.D.A.)	1 oz.
Protein	4
Vitamin C	45
Vitamin B	45
Niacin	45
Calcium	2
Iron	15
Zinc	10

58. The graph below provides a breakdown of retail sales for 2007.   58._____
Based on this data, at least, what
percent of the total retail sales are
spent on items related to cars?

A. 7.3%
B. 16.6%
C. 19.3%
D. 26.6%

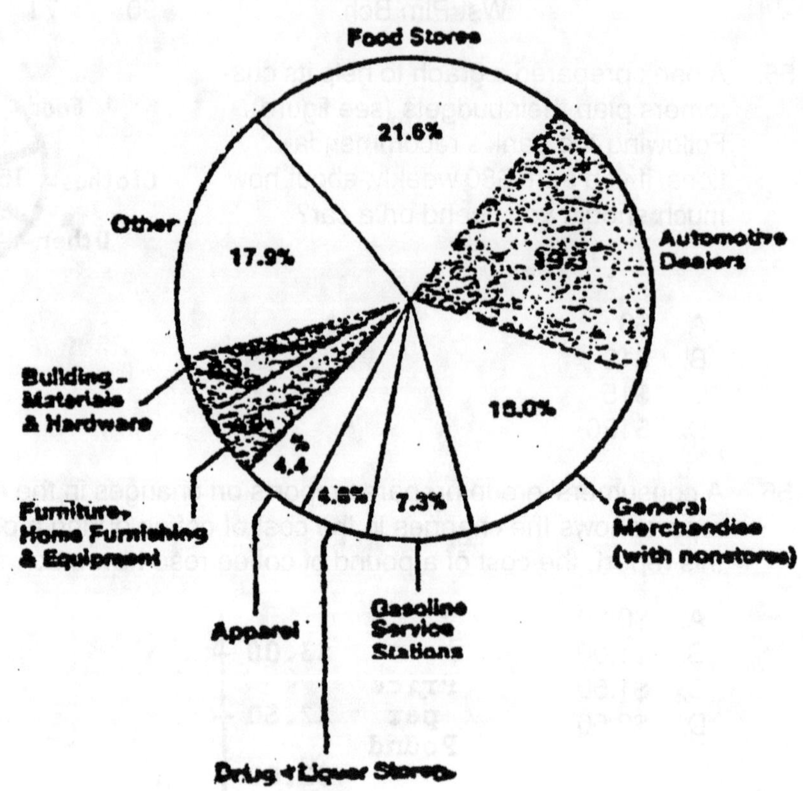

59. Riverview High School prepared a monthly report on absences.   59._____
During which week was
there the *GREATEST*
increase in the number of
students absent from
school?

A. First
B. Second
C. Third
D. Fourth

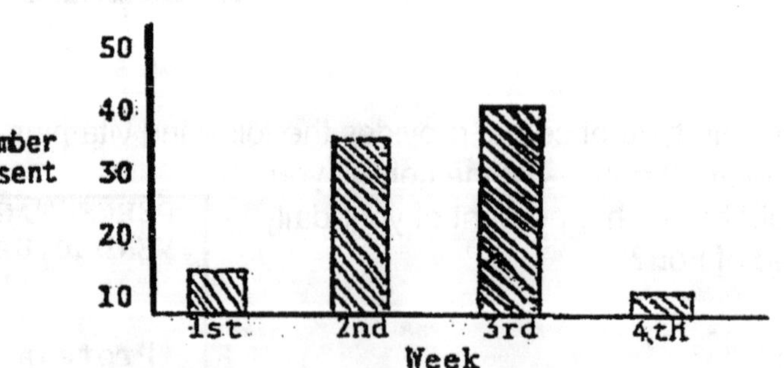

EDUCATION LEVEL ATTAINED BY HIGH SCHOOL STUDENTS
ENTERING HIGH SCHOOL IN 2010 AND 2011

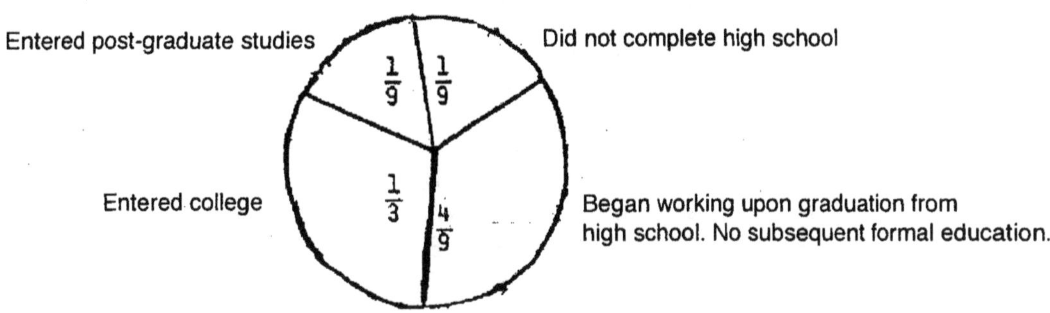

ENTERING CLASS OF 2010 – TOTAL OF 117

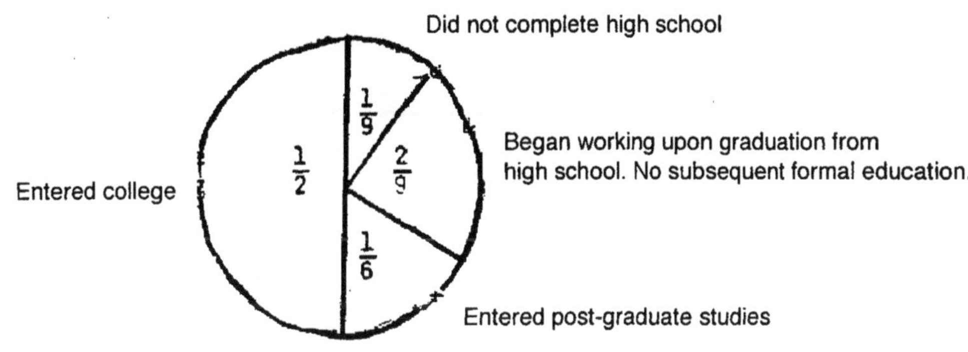

ENTERING CLASS OF 2011 – TOTAL OF 180

60. The total number of students from both classes who went to work immediately after high   60.____
school graduation was

   A. 33   B. 40   C. 92   D. 129

KEY (CORRECT ANSWERS)

1.	B	16.	C	31.	D	46.	B
2.	C	17.	B	32.	C	47.	B
3.	B	18.	B	33.	B	48.	B
4.	C	19.	D	34.	C	49.	B
5.	C	20.	A	35.	B	50.	B
6.	C	21.	B	36.	C	51.	C
7.	C	22.	A	37.	B	52.	A
8.	A	23.	D	38.	A	53.	C
9.	C	24.	B	39.	B	54.	D
10.	D	25.	B	40.	B	55.	B
11.	B	26.	D	41.	C	56.	B
12.	D	27.	C	42.	C	57.	C
13.	C	28.	D	43.	C	58.	D
14.	D	29.	C	44.	B	59.	B
15.	A	30.	B	45.	C	60.	C

MATHEMATICS
SOLUTIONS TO PROBLEMS

1. Answer: B. 6 hours, 25 minutes

<u>SOLUTION</u>

1.	7:45 A.M. to 8:00 A.M.	=		15 min.
2.	8:00 A.M. to 2:00 P.M.	=	6 hours	
3.	2:00 P.M. to 2:10 P.M.	=		10 min.
4.	(Adding)		6 hours,	25 min

2. Answer: C. 4 hours, 50 minutes

<u>SOLUTION</u>

1. Look under the heading, Departures. The next bus to Tallahassee is scheduled to leave at 1:20 P.M.
2. 8:30 A.M. to 1:20 P.M. = 4 hours, 50 minutes

3. Answer: B. 1 day 17 hours 10 minutes

<u>SOLUTION</u>

1. 3:20 P.M., 13 Nov to 3:20 P.M., 15 Nov = 2 days = 48 hrs
2. 8:30 A.M. to 3:20 P.M. = 6 hours, 5O minutes
3. 48 hours - 6 hours, 50 minutes = 41 hours, 10 minutes
4. 41 hours, 10 minutes = 1 day, 17 hours, 10 minutes

4. Answer: C. April 1, 2013   4.____

<u>SOLUTION</u>

1. 30 months = 2 years, 6 months
2. 10/1/10 + 2 years = 10/1/12
3. 10/1 + 6 months = 4/1/13
4. That is, 4/1/13

5. Answer: C. $29.52   5.____

<u>SOLUTION</u>

$25.00	(1 ten, 3 five-dollar bills)
2.00	(2 one-dollar bills)
1.00	(2 50-cent pieces)
1.25	(5 quarters)
.20	(2 dimes)
.05	(1 nickel)
.02	(2 pennies)
$29.52	

6. Answer: C. Six dollars - two quarters - two pennies   6.____

<u>SOLUTION</u>

1. $10.00 - $3.48 = $6.52
2. $ 6.52 = six dollars, two quarters - two pennies

7. Answer: C. 2 pennies, 1 nickel, 1 dime, 1 quarter, 2 dollar bills, 2 five-dollar bills   7.____

SOLUTION

1. $20.00 - $7.58 = $12.42
2. $12.42 = 2 pennies, 1 nickel, 1 dime, 1 quarter, two dollar bills, 2 five-dollar bills

8. Answer: A.   8.____

SOLUTION

A. $40.00 - $28.73 = $11.27
B. $11.27 = one ten-dollar bill, one dollar, 1 quarter, 2 pennies (Answer A)

9. Answer: C. 50   9.____

SOLUTION

1. Divide 685 by 14, thus:

2.
$$14\overline{)\begin{array}{r} 48 \\ 685 \\ \underline{56} \\ 125 \\ \underline{112} \\ 13 \end{array}}$$

3. 48 13/14 is nearest to 50

10. Answer: D. 800   10.____

SOLUTION

1. 16 X 2 (2 stories) = 32 classrooms
2. Multiply 32 X 25, thus:

3.
$$\begin{array}{r} 32 \\ \times 25 \\ \hline 160 \\ 64 \\ \hline 800 \end{array}$$

11. Answer: B. 10 hours   11.____

SOLUTION

1. Divide 30,000 by 50 = 600 (minutes)
2. 600 (minutes) divided by 60 (60 minutes to an hour) = 10 hours

12. Answer: D. 198   12.____

SOLUTION

1. 3 buckets = 45
2. 5 barrels = 105
3. 1 tub = 48/198

13. Answer: C. 127   13.____

SOLUTION

1. Add: 12 - 1 Van
        60 - 2 Coaches
        55 - 1 Bus
       ___
       127

14. Answer: D. $6696   14.____

SOLUTION

1. $6200 X .08 = $496.00
2. $6200 + $496 = $6696

15. Answer: A. 23.0   15.____

SOLUTION

1. Divide 1436 by 62.4, thus:

2. $62.4\sqrt{1436.0}$
         23.0
         1248
         ____
         1880
         1872
         ____
            8

16. Answer: C. $23.58   16.____

SOLUTION

1. 14.5 X .69 = $10.01
2. 23.0 X .59 = 13.57
3. (Adding) $23.58
WORK:

1.   14.5   2.   23
    X   .69   X .59
        ____   ____
        1305   207
         870   115
        ______   ____
      10.005 = $10.01 $13.57

17. Answer: B. 27.6 inches   17.____

SOLUTION

1. 30 X .08 = 2.4
2. 30 - 2.4 = 27.6 (Answer B)

18. Answer: B. $0.69   18.____

SOLUTION

1. $29.90 + $1.87 = $31.77
2. $5.41 X 6 = $32.46
3. $32.46 - 31.77 = $ .69

19. Answer: D. Car Care Center - Regular price $40. Sale $29.50.   19.____

A. $40 (1st tire)
    $20 (2nd tire)
    $40 (3rd tire)
    $20 (4th tire)
    $120

B. $40 X 1/4 = $10
    $40 - $10 = $30
    $30 X 4 = $120

C. $40 X 3 = 120
    4th tire =   0
               $120

D. $29.50
           X 4
         $118.00

20. Answer: A. nothing

20.____

<u>SOLUTION</u>

1. $69.96
       + 1. 98
        $71.94

2. $11.99
          x 6
        $71.94

21. Answer: B. Large

21.____

<u>SOLUTION</u>

1. $.40 ÷ 12 = .03 1/3
2. .60 ÷ 20 = .03
3. .95 ÷ 30 = .03 1/4
4. .95 ÷ 60 = .03 1/4

22. Answer: A. $ .10

22.____

<u>SOLUTION</u>

1. 4 dozens = 48
2. 48 = 6 x .65 = $3.90
3. 48 = 4 X .95 = $3.80
4. $3.90 - $3.80 = $0.10 (saving)

23. Answer: D. $864

23.____

<u>SOLUTION</u>

1. $800 X .08 = $ 64
2. $800 + $64 = $864

24. Answer: B. $190

24.____

<u>SOLUTION</u>

1. $3800 X .05 = $190

25. Answer: B. $3.00

25.____

<u>SOLUTION</u>

A. 12 months / 3 months = 1/4
B. 1/4 X .06 = .015
C. $200 X .015 = $3.00

26. Answer: D. $750

26.____

<u>SOLUTION</u>

1. $3000 - $500 = $2500 (unpaid balance)
2. $2500 X .10 X 3 = $750

27. Answer: C. $927

27.____

<u>SOLUTION</u>

1. $1300 - $400 = $900
2. 6% per annum = 3% for six months
3. $900 X .03 = $27
4. $900 + $27 = $927

28. Answer: D. $6.76

28.____

<u>SOLUTION</u>

1. Tax on first dollar   = $.04
2. Tax on five whole dollars = .20
3. Tax on .50   = .02
4. Total tax   = .26
5. Cost of dinner   = $6.76

29. Answer: C. $ 294.00

29.____

<u>SOLUTION</u>

1. Daily sales tax = 40 X .04 = $1.60
2. Daily resort tax = 40 X .01 = $ .40
3. $40 + $1.60 + $.40 = $42.00/day. Then, (42)(7) = $294.00/week

30. Answer: B. $10.28

30.____

<u>SOLUTION</u>

1. Sales Tax: On $9   = $ .36
             On $.88 = $ .04
                       $ .40
2. $9.88 + $.40 = $10.28

31. Answer: D. $36,400

31.____

<u>SOLUTION</u>

1. $35,000 X .04 = $1,400
2. $35,000 + $1,400 = $36,400

32. Answer: C. $4,680

32.____

<u>SOLUTION</u>

1. $4,500 savings   = $4,500
2. +4,500 x .04   = $180
3. $4,500 + $180   = $4,680 (total savings)

33. Answers B. $10

33._____

<u>SOLUTION</u>

1. $15. X 1/3 = $5
2. 2 X $5 = $10

34. Answer: B. $31.20

34._____

<u>SOLUTION</u>

1. $25 X .80 = $20.00
2. $4 X .80 = 3.20
3. $10 .80 = 10.00 (no "discount; not tenolsr equipment)
    $33.20

35. Answer: B. $180.60

35._____

<u>SOLUTION</u>

1. $258 X .70 = $180.60

36. Answer: C. $33.50

36._____

<u>SOLUTION</u>

1. Shirt: $10 X .75 = $ 7.50
2. Jeans: $15 X 2/3 = $10.00
3. Sweater: $24 X 2/3 = $16.00
    $33.50

37. Answer: B. 13 yards

37._____

<u>SOLUTION</u>

1. 8 X 55 = 440 inches
2. 440 ÷ 36 = 12 8/36 = 12 2/9 yards

38. Answer: A. 176 yards

38._____

<u>SOLUTION</u>

1. 1760 yards 10 = 176 yards

39. Answer: B. 1.21 meters

39._____

<u>SOLUTION</u>

1. 4 X 30.4 cm = 121.6 cm
2. 121.6 cm = 1.216 meters

40. Answer: B. 30.4 meters

40._____

<u>SOLUTION</u>

1. 2.28 kilometers = 2280 meters
2. 2280 ÷ 75 = 30.4 meters

WORK:
$$75\,\overline{)2280.0}^{\,30.4}$$

$$\begin{array}{r} 225 \\ \hline 300 \\ \underline{300} \end{array}$$

41. Answer: C. $2.85   41.____

<u>SOLUTION</u>

1. Area of rectangle = 1 X W
2. 40 X 3 1/3 = 40 X 10/3 = 400/3 = 133,33 square yards

42. Answer: C. 480 meters   42.____

<u>SOLUTION</u>

A.

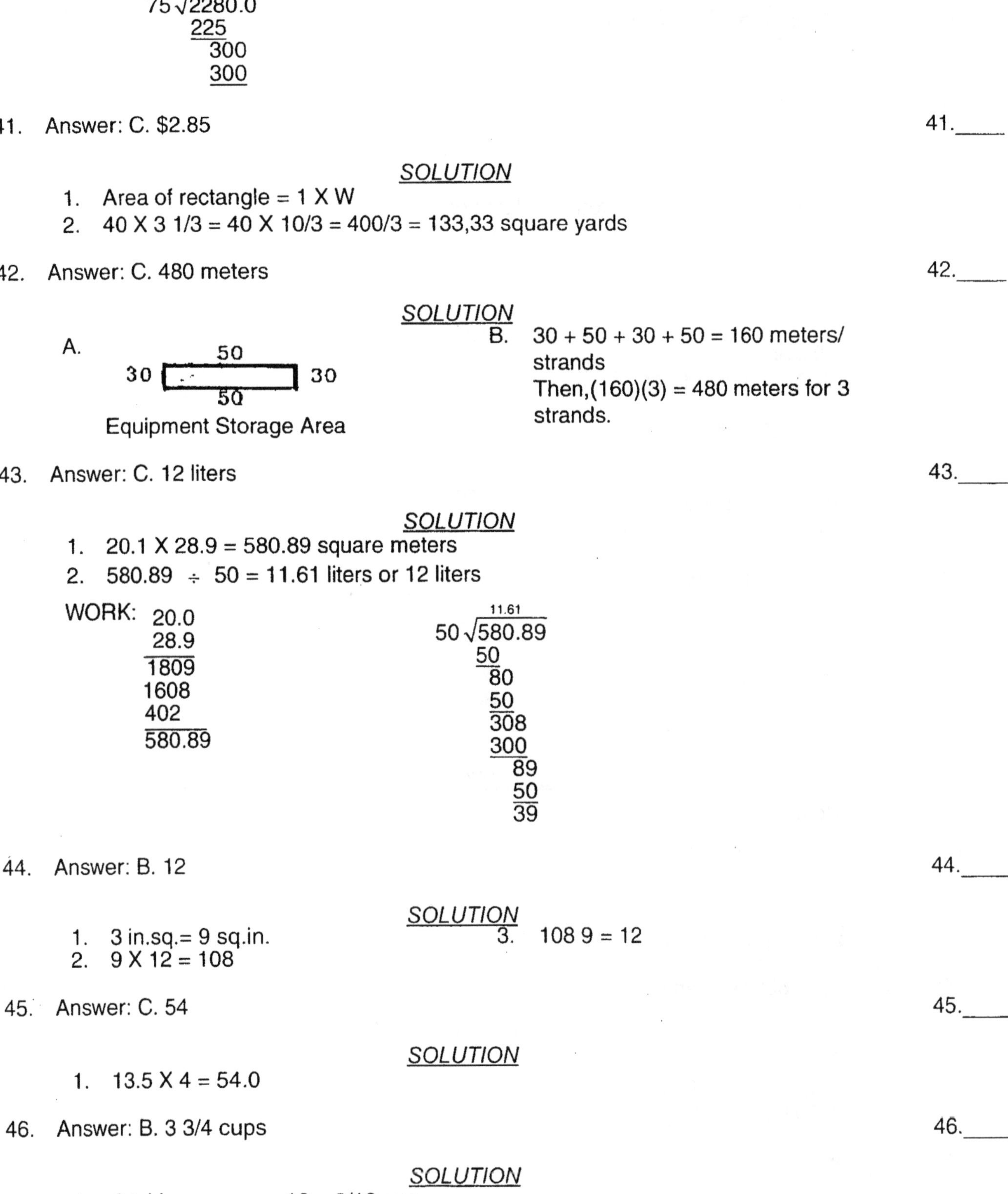

B. 30 + 50 + 30 + 50 = 160 meters/ strands
Then,(160)(3) = 480 meters for 3 strands.

43. Answer: C. 12 liters   43.____

<u>SOLUTION</u>

1. 20.1 X 28.9 = 580.89 square meters
2. 580.89 ÷ 50 = 11.61 liters or 12 liters

WORK:
$$\begin{array}{r} 20.0 \\ 28.9 \\ \hline 1809 \\ 1608 \\ 402 \\ \hline 580.89 \end{array}$$

$$50\,\overline{)580.89}^{\,11.61}$$

$$\begin{array}{r} 50 \\ \hline 80 \\ 50 \\ \hline 308 \\ 300 \\ \hline 89 \\ 50 \\ \hline 39 \end{array}$$

44. Answer: B. 12   44.____

<u>SOLUTION</u>

1. 3 in.sq.= 9 sq.in.
2. 9 X 12 = 108
3. 108 9 = 12

45. Answer: C. 54   45.____

<u>SOLUTION</u>

1. 13.5 X 4 = 54.0

46. Answer: B. 3 3/4 cups   46.____

<u>SOLUTION</u>

1. 3 tablespoons ÷ 16 = 3/16 cup

$$2. \quad \cancel{20}^{\;5} \times \frac{3}{\cancel{16}_{\;4}} = 15/4 = 3\ 3/4 \text{ cups}$$

47. Answer: B. 15 liters

47._____

SOLUTION

1. 200 ml = 1/5 liter
2. 1/5 liter motor oil is required for 3 liters of gasoline
3. Therefore, 1 liter will require 5X3 liters of gasoline or 15 liters

48. Answer: B. 17

48._____

SOLUTION

1. 2.5 liters = 2,500 ml
2. 2500 ÷ 150 = 16.60

49. Answer: B. 2.5 tons

49._____

SOLUTION

1. 1000 X 5 = 5000
2. 5000 ÷ 2000. = 2.5 tons

50. Answer: B. a little more tnan 3 ozs.

50._____

SOLUTION

1. 20 X 16 = 320 ozs.
2. 320 ÷ 100 = 3.2

51. Answer: C. 2.5 metric tons

51._____

SOLUTION

A. Boat: 1350 kg

B. Motor: 425 kg

C. Trailer: 725 kg
         2500 kg

D. 2500 kg = 2.5 metric tons

52. Answer: A. 600 kilograms

52._____

SOLUTION

1. 60 X 40 = 2400 kg
2. 3 X 1000 = 3000 kg
3. 3000 kg - 240.0 kg = 600 kg

53. Answer: C. $46.41

53._____

SOLUTION

1. $43.20 + $3.21 = $46.41

54. Answer: D. Orlando   54._____

SOLUTION

   1. Orlando - 94° (by inspection)

55. Answer: B. $12   55._____

SOLUTION

   1. Transportation - 15%
   2. $80 X .15 = $12

56. Answer: B. $1.00   56._____

SOLUTION

   1. April 1 - $1.50
   2. July 1 - $2.50
   3. $2.50 - $1.50 = $1.00

57. Answer: C. 30%   57._____

SOLUTION

   1. 15% X 2 = 30%

58. Answer: D. 26.6%   58._____

SOLUTION

   1. Automotive dealers - 19.3%
   2. Gasoline service stations - 7.3%/26.6%

59. Answer: B. Second   59._____

SOLUTION

   1. Second (by inspection)

60. Answer: C. 92   60._____

SOLUTION

   1. $\frac{4}{\cancel{9}} \times \cancel{117}^{13} = 52$ (2010)

   2. $\frac{2}{\cancel{9}} \times \cancel{180}^{20} = 40$ (2011)

   3. 52+40 = 92

BASIC MATHEMATICS
EXAMINATION SECTION
TEST 1

DIRECTIONS: Each question or incomplete statement is followed by several suggested answers or completions. Select the one that BEST answers the question or completes the statement. *PRINT THE LETTER OF THE CORRECT ANSWER IN THE SPACE AT THE RIGHT.*

1. Add: 5,796 + 6 + 243 + 24   1._____

   A. 6,069   B. 6,079   C. 6,169   D. 6,179

2. Subtract: 8,007 - 6,898   2._____

   A. 1,109   B. 1,119   C. 1,209   D. 2,109

3. Multiply: 3,876 x 904   3._____

   A. 364,344   B. 3,493,904
   C. 3,494,904   D. 3,503,904

                                                                                 4._____
4. Divide: $76\sqrt{58,976}$

   A. 775   B. 776   C. 786   D. 876

5. Combine: (+4) + (-3) - (-7)   5._____

   A. -6   B. +6   C. +8   D. +14

6. Simplify: [(-8) x (-6)] ÷ (-3)   6._____

   A. -16   B. -14   C. +14   D. +16

7. Add: 1 3/5 + 3 7/8   7._____

   A. 4 10/40   B. 4 10/13   C. 4 19/40   D. 5 19/40

8. Subtract: 4 3/8 - 2 2/3   8._____

   A. 1 17/24   B. 2 1/24   C. 2 1/5   D. 2 17/24

9. Multiply: 3 2/3 x 5 1/2   9._____

   A. 15 1/3   B. 16 1/3   C. 20 1/6   D. 21 1/6

                                                                                 10._____
10. Divide: $7\frac{1}{2} \div 2\frac{1}{4}$

    A. 3/10   B. 3 1/3   C. 3 1/2   D. 16 7/8

11. Add: 434.7 + .04 + 7.107   11._____

    A. .441847   B. .442207   C. 441.847   D. 442.207

12. Subtract: 986.4 - 34.87   12.____

    A. 6.377   B. 63.77   C. 951.53   D. 9,515.3

13. Multiply: 5.96   13.____
$$\times 87.4$$

    A. 51.0904   B. 52.0904   C. 510.904   D. 520.904

14. Divide: $.034\sqrt{6.698}$ 14.____

    A. 19.2   B. 19.7   C. 192   D. 197

15. Add: $.7 + \dfrac{1}{2}$ 15.____

    A. .12   B. 1.2   C. 7/2   D. 15/2

16. What is 5.5% of 75?   16.____

    A. 4.125   B. 13.65   C. 41.25   D. 412.5

17. 12 is what percent of 6?   17.____

    A. $\dfrac{1}{2}\%$ B. 5%   C. 50%   D. 200%

18. 14 is 28% of ______.   18.____

    A. 2   B. 5   C. 50   D. 500

19. A record player sells for $92.00. It is discounted 15% for a special sale. What is the sale price?   19.____

    A. $13.80   B. $68.20   C. $77.00   D. $78.20

20.   20.____

Table A - Acme Mortgage Company
$320 Loan - 3/4 of 1% Interest

Month	Payment	Principal Paid/Month	Interest Paid/Month
1	$ 27.98	$ 25.58	$ 2.40
2	27.98	25.77	2.21
3	27.98	25.96	2.02
4	27.98	26.15	1.83
5	27.98	26.35	1.63
6	27.98	26.55	1.43
7	27.98	26.75	1.23
8	27.98	26.95	1.03
9	27.98	27.15	.83
10	27.98	27.35	.63
11	27.98	27.56	.42
12	27.93	27.77	.16
Total	$335.82	$ 320.00	$ 15.82

Acme Mortgage Company charges 3/4 of 1% (.0075) on the unpaid balance per month. Bowman Mortgage Company charges 9% per year on the total loan. Which company charges the LEAST amount of interest on a $320 loan held for one year?

   A. Acme charges the least amount.
   B. Bowman charges the least amount.
   C. Acme and Bowman charge the same.
   D. Insufficient information to determine.

21.   Percent of Auto Insurance Discounts for   21.____
High School Students with Certain
Grade Point Averages

Policy Coverage	Grade Point Averages Percent of Discount		
	A	B	C
Liability	33 1/3%	33 1/3%	10%
Comprehensive	20%	10%	-
Collision	25%	20%	-

Frank Verna has a B average. The regular 6-month amounts to be paid for insurance before discount follow:

Liability	$18.00
Comprehensive	$20.00
Collision	$60.00
Total	$98.00

How much does Frank pay for insurance for 6 months?

   A. $20.00   B. $58.00   C. $78.00   D. $156.00

22. Mr. Martinez had a fire in his home. Repairing the damage will cost about $900. His   22.____
home is valued at $14,000 and is insured for $12,000. Mr. Martinez had paid $32.00 a year for ten years for his insurance. The insurance company has agreed to pay the full amount of the claim ($900).
Which of the following statements are TRUE?
     I. The amount of the claim is more than what has been paid to the company.
    II. The insurance company should pay $14,000 for this claim.
   III. If the house had been completely burned, the insurance company would pay $14,000.
   IV. The maximum claim Mr. Martinez could collect is $12,000
The CORRECT answer is:

   A. I, II   B. I, III   C. II, III   D. I, IV

23. When two coins are tossed, what is the chance that both will be heads?   23.____
1 in

   A. 1   B. 2   C. 3   D. 4

24. If 4 teams are in a football league, how many games are necessary to allow each team to   24.____
play every team one time? ______ games.

   A. 6   B. 9   C. 12   D. 16

25. Five people donated money to the Red Cross. The donations were: $52.00, $76.00, $18.00, $94.00, and $120.00.
What was the AVERAGE donation?

   A. $70   B. $72   C. $76   D. $360

25.____

26. From the following statements, determine the CORRECT conclusion.
    I. If Lauraine is a red-head, then Lauraine is hot-tempered.
    II. Lauraine is not hot-tempered.
The CORRECT answer is:

   A. Lauraine is a red-head.
   B. Lauraine is not a red-head.
   C. Lauraine could be a red-head.
   D. All red-heads are hot-tempered.

26.____

27. The graph represents the way the Jones family spends its money (budget). What is the monthly income if they are spending $4080 per year for food?

   A. $1,020
   B. $1,360
   C. $4,080
   D. $16,320

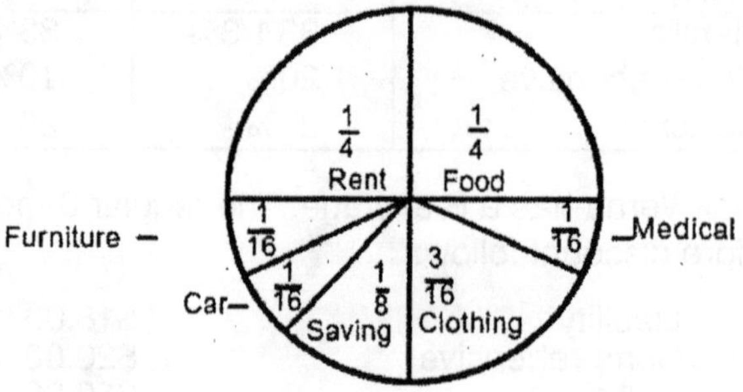

$\frac{1}{4}$ Rent | $\frac{1}{4}$ Food | Furniture — $\frac{1}{16}$ | $\frac{1}{16}$ Medical | Car — $\frac{1}{16}$ | $\frac{1}{8}$ Saving | $\frac{3}{16}$ Clothing

27.____

28.

	S	M	T	W	T	F	S
Charlie Simms	?	8	8	8	8	8	3
Jim Chow	2	9	8	8	9	9	4

Time and one-half is paid on Saturdays and for hours worked beyond 8 hours each day. Double-time is paid for Sunday work.
Mr. Simms would have to work how many hours on Sunday to earn as much as Mr. Chow?

        Regular time - $2.00/hour
        Time and one-half - $3.00/hour
        Double time - $4.00/hour

______ hours.

   A. 2   B. 5   C. 6   D. 20

28.____

29. Jane Gunther wrote checks for these items:
    $16.95 for a hair dryer
    $125.50 for a car payment
    $33.68 for television repair
    $21.59 for a dress
Jane had a beginning check balance (before she wrote the checks) of $351.76. She also deposited $41.50 into her account.
After the checks were written and the deposit made, what was her new balance?

   A. $154.04   B. $195.54   C. $196.54   D. $239.22

29.____

30. Given the formula I = PRT:
    If I = 24, R = .05, T = 3, find P.

    A. .00625 B. 1.6 C. 3.6 D. 160.0

30._____

31. Fencing is needed to enclose a piece of
    land 26 meters on a side.
    How much fencing is needed?
    _______ meters.
    A. 52
    B. 98
    C. 104
    D. 676

31._____

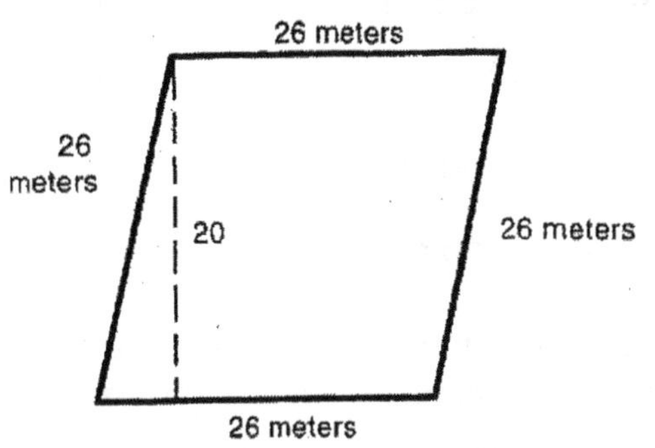

32. The area of figure A is 12 square units, and the
    area of B is 18 square units.
    What is the area of figure C?
    _______ square units.
    A. 16
    B. 16 1/2
    C. 17
    D. 17 1/2

32._____

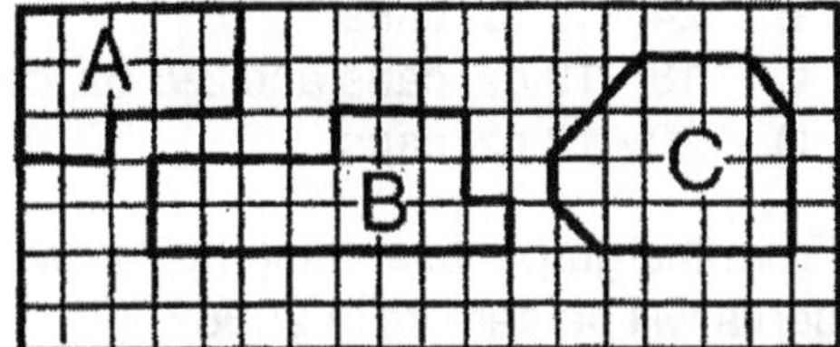

33. Using a 3 gallon spray can with a mixture rate of 1 teaspoon of insecticide per quart of
    water and an application rate of 1 gallon of mixture per 100 square feet, how much water
    and how much insecticide will be needed to spray an 85 feet by 10 feet lawn?
    _______ teaspoons of insecticide and _______ gallons of water.

    A. 34; 8 1/2 B. 34; 11 C. 17; 8 1/2 D. 24; 6

33._____

34. Bill Mata will carpet his living room which has the fol-
    lowing dimensions. If Bill pays $6.00 per square yard
    for the carpet, how much will it cost to carpet his living
    room?
    (9 square feet = 1 square yard)
    A. $192
    B. $216
    C. $1,728
    D. $1,944

34._____

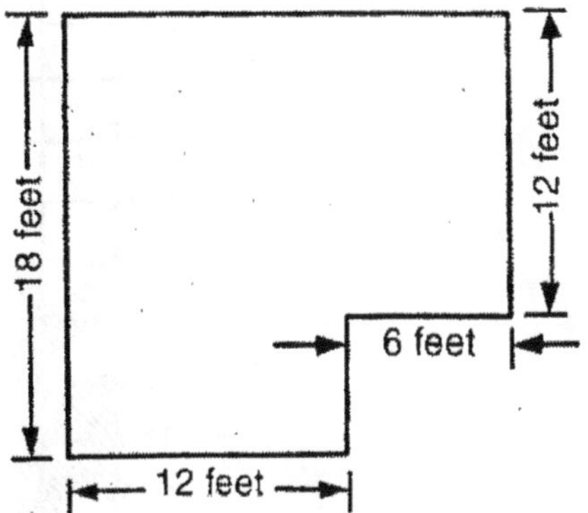

35. A cube is painted red and then divided into 27 smaller cubes.
    How many of the smaller cubes are painted on one side only?
    A. 4
    B. 6
    C. 8
    D. 10

35._____

36. John and Frank wish to pour a cement walk 108 feet long, 4 feet wide, and 3 inches deep.
If ready-mix concrete can be delivered on weekdays for $19.50 a cubic yard and on weekends for $22.50 a cubic yard, how much would they save on the complete job if they decide on Thursday rather than on the weekend? (1 cubic yard = 27 cubic feet)

    A. $3.00   B. $12.00   C. $36.00   D. $78.00

36.____

37. Antifreeze may be purchased in different size containers for different prices:
        8 oz. can - 43¢
        10 oz. can - 51¢
        12 oz. can - 62¢
If exactly 15 pints of antifreeze are needed, how many cans of each size are needed for the cost to be minimum? (16 oz. = 1 pint)

    A. 12 - 10 oz. cans and 10 - 12 oz. cans
    B. 24 - 10 oz. cans
    C. 18 - 12 oz. cans and 3-8 oz. cans
    D. 20 - 12 oz. cans

37.____

38. From the graph, assuming the growth rate in the senior class is constant, how many students will be seniors in 2006?

    A. 225
    B. 250
    C. 300
    D. 375

38.____

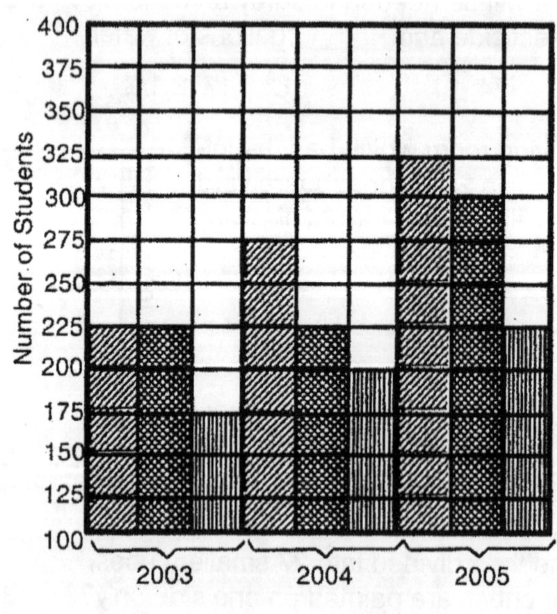

39.   39.____

Population in U.S.
1880-1980

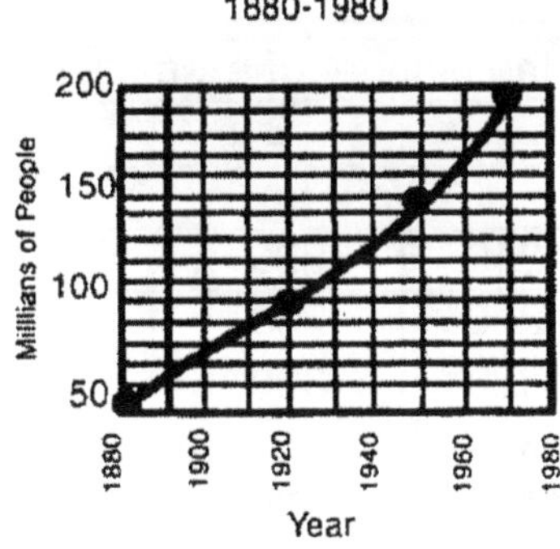

Percentage of the U.S.
Population Over 65

In looking at the two graphs, which of the following conclusions are TRUE?
- I. Both graphs show population growth.
- II. Both graphs cover exactly the same time period.
- III. The percentage of *over 65* population remains the same over the 1940 to 1970 period.
- IV. If you were in the retail business, you might expect greater sales to the *over 65* population in 1970 than in 1940.
- V. In the general population of about 200 million people in 1970, 24 million were over 65.
- VI. In 1920, there were only about 7 million people *over 65* out of about 100 million people.

The CORRECT answer is:

   A. I, III, IV   B. II, IV, V
   C. II, III, VI   D. I, IV, V

40. Jerry Martin owns a home with a market value of $180,000. Its assessed value is 25% of   40.____
the market value. The tax rate is $5.00 per $100 of assessed value.
What is the amount of his tax?

   A. $225.00   B. $2,250.00   C. $4,500.00   D. $6,750.00

41. You are governor of the state and you need an additional 500 million dollars in tax   41.____
money. To raise the money, an increase in sales tax is required.
What information would be MOST helpful in determining the new tax rate?
- I. Average income per person in the state
- II. Number of people out of work
- III. Population of the state over 18 years of age
- IV. Birth rate in the state
- V. Percent of income spent on taxable goods
- VI. Percent of income spent on non-taxable goods
- VII. Number of people filing income tax returns

The CORRECT answer is:

   A. I, IV, VI   B. II, III, VII
   C. V, VI   D. I, V

42. 42._____

Income Tax Table

If adjusted gross income is-		And the number of exemptions is -					
		1	2	3	4	5	6
At least	But less than	Your tax is -					
$24,500	$24,750	$2360	$1240	$230	$0	$0	$0
24,750	25,000	2400	1280	260	0	0	0
25,000	25,250	2440	1320	300	0	0	0
25,250	25.500	2480	1360	330	0	0	0
25,500	25,750	2530	1390	370	0	0	0
25,750	26,000	2570	1430	400	0	0	0
26,000	26,250	2610	1470	440	0	0	0
26,250	26,500	2650	1510	470	0	0	0
26,500	26,750	2700	1550	510	0	0	0
26,750	27,000	2740	1590	540	0	0	0
27,000	27,250	2780	1630	580	0	0	0
27,250	27,500	2820	1670	610	0	0	0
27,500	27,750	2870	1710	650	0	0	0
27,750	28 000	2910	1750	680	0	0	0
28,000	28,250	2950	1790	720	0	0	0
28,250	28,500	2990	1830	760	0	0	0
28,500	28,750	3040	1870	790	0	0	0

Jerry Ladd earned $28,390.00 during the year. To find his adjusted gross income, he must reduce the amount earned by the standard 10% deduction. He had only one exemption, himself.
How much tax did Jerry pay?

A. $1390   B. $1830   C. $2530   D. $2990

43. 43._____

Weight in Ounces	2 oz.	4 oz .	12 oz.	21 oz.
Price	5¢	7¢	15¢	24¢

Using the above table, predict the price if the weight is 32 ounces.

A. 27¢   B. 28¢   C. 29¢   D. 35¢

44. Given [(0,2), (1,4), (2,6),...(5,y)].
What is the value of y? 44._____

A. 8   B. 10   C. 12   D. 14

45. If the larger of two numbers is two and one-half times the smaller number, what fraction is the smaller of the larger? 45._____

A. 3/4   B. 4/5   C. 5/8   D. 2/5

46. John can save 75¢ a week. He has $3.75 in the bank now. How many weeks will it take him to have a total deposit of $12? 46._____

A. 16   B. 9   C. 11   D. 17

47. Using the approximation of 3.14 for pi, find the area of a circle whose diameter is 20 inches.

      _______ square inches.

    A. 31.4   B. 314   C. 628   D. 1256

47.____

48. Express .045 as a percent.

    A. 45%   B. 4.5%   C. .45%   D. .045%

48.____

49. Twenty is what percent of 50?

    A. 40   B. 60   C. 25   D. 16 2/3

49.____

50. Two hundred twenty-five percent of 160 is

    A. 80   B. 350   C. 360   D. 440

50.____

KEY (CORRECT ANSWERS)

1. A	11. C	21. C	31. C	41. C
2. A	12. C	22. D	32. C	42. C
3. D	13. D	23. D	33. A	43. D
4. B	14. D	24. A	34. A	44. C
5. C	15. B	25. B	35. B	45. D
6. A	16. A	26. B	36. B	46. C
7. D	17. D	27. D	37. B	47. B
8. A	18. C	28. B	38. B	48. B
9. C	19. D	29. B	39. D	49. A
10. B	20. A	30. D	40. B	50. C

SOLUTIONS TO PROBLEMS

1. $5796 + 6 + 243 + 24 = 6069$

2. $8007 - 6898 = 1109$

3. $(3876)(904) = 3,503,904$

4. $58,976 \div 76 = 776$

5. $(+4) + (-3) - (-7) = 4 - 3 + 7 = +8$

6. $[(-8)(-6)] \div -3 = 48 \div -3 = -16$

7. $1\frac{3}{5} + 3\frac{7}{8} = 1\frac{24}{40} + 3\frac{35}{40} = 4\frac{59}{40} = 5\frac{19}{40}$

8. $4\frac{3}{8} - 2\frac{2}{3} = 4\frac{9}{24} - 2\frac{16}{24} = 3\frac{33}{24} - 2\frac{16}{24} = 1\frac{17}{24}$

9. $(3\frac{2}{3})(5\frac{1}{2}) = (\frac{11}{3})(\frac{11}{2}) = \frac{121}{6} = 20\frac{1}{6}$

10. $7\frac{1}{2} \div 2\frac{1}{4} = \frac{15}{2} \div \frac{9}{4} = (\frac{15}{2})(\frac{4}{9}) = \frac{60}{18} = 3\frac{1}{3}$

11. $434.7 + .04 + 7.107 = 441.847$

12. $986.4 - 34.87 = 951.53$

13. $(5.96)(87.4) = 520.904$

14. $6.698 \div .034 = 197$

15. $.7 + \frac{1}{2} = .7 + .5 = 1.2$

16. $(.055)(75) = 4.125$

17. $\frac{12}{6} = 2 = 200\%$

18. $14 \div .28 = 50$

19. $\$92 - (.15)(\$92) = \$78.20$

20. Acme's interest charge = $\$15.82$, whereas Bowman's interest charge = $(.09)(\$320) = \$28.80$. Thus, Acme charges less.

21. $(\$18.00)(66\frac{2}{3}\%) + (\$20.00)(90\%) + (\$60.00)(80\%) = \$78.00$

22. Statements I and IV are correct. For 10 years, he has paid \$320, but collected \$900 on his claim. Also, since the insured value of the home is \$12,000, he could not collect more than that amount on any claim.

23. Probability of 2 heads = (1/2) (1/2) = 1/4, which means 1 in 4.

24. The number of required games = (4)(3) ÷ 2 = 6

25. Average donation = (\$52.00 + \$76.00 + \$18.00 + \$94.00 + \$120.00) ÷ 5 = \$72

26. The correct conclusion is B: Lauraine is not a redhead. Let p = Lauraine is a redhead, q = Lauraine is hot-tempered. The given statement says: *If p, then q.* The contrapositive, which is also true, says, *If not q, then not p.* This corresponds to statement B.

27. Let x = monthly income. Then, \$4080 = Solving, x = \$16,320.

28. Mr. Chow's earnings = (2)(\$4) + (40)(\$2) + (7)(\$3) = \$109.
For Monday through Saturday, Mr. Simms' earnings =
(40)(\$2) + (3)(\$3) = \$89. Thus, Mr. Simms would need to earn
109 - 89 = \$20 on Sunday. This means Sunday's time =
\$20 ÷ \$4 = 5 hours.

29. New balance = \$351.76 + \$41.50 - \$16.95 - \$125.50 - \$33.68 -\$21.59 = \$195.54.

30. 24 = (P)(.05)(3), 24 = .15P, so P = 160

31. Fencing: (26)(4) = 104 meters.

32. Area of $C = (4)(5) - (\frac{1}{2})(1)(1) - (\frac{1}{2})(2)(2) - (\frac{1}{2})(1)(1) = 17$

33. (85)(10) = 850 sq.ft. = 8.5 gallons of water. Now, 8.5 gallons = 34 quarts, so 34 teaspoons of insecticide are needed.

34. Area = (12)(6) + (12)(18) = 288 sq.ft. = 32 sq.yds. Total cost = (32)(\$6) = \$192

35. There are 6 cubes painted red on only one side. They are found in the center of each face of the original cube.

36. $(108)(4)(\frac{1}{4}) = 108$ cu.ft. = 4 cu.yds. Savings would be (\$22.50)(4) - (\$19.50)(4) = \$12.00

37. 15 pints = 240 oz. The costs for each selection are:
For A: (12)(.51) + (10)(.62) = \$12.32; for B: (24)(.51) = \$12.24; for
C: (18)(.62) + (3)(.43) = \$12.45; for D: (20)(.62) = \$12.40.
So, selection B is the minimum cost.

38. The number of seniors in 2003, 2004, 2005 are 175, 200, and 225, respectively. If growth is constant, the number of seniors in 2006 is 250.

39. Statements I, IV, V are correct. Statement II is wrong because the 1st graph covers 1800-1970, whereas the 2nd graph covers 1940-1970. Statement III is wrong because the *over 65* population increases in percent from 7% in 1940 to 12% in 1970.

40. (25%)($180,000) = $45,000 assessed value. Amount of tax = ($5.00)($45,000 ÷ $100) = $2,250

41. For increasing sales tax, it would be helpful in knowing the respective percent of incor spent on taxable vs. non-taxable goods.

42. Adjusted gross income = ($28390)(.90) = $25551.00. On the tax chart, this figure lies between $25500 and $25750. Using the column for 1 exemption, the tax is $2530.

43. Using 2 oz. = .05, note that each additional oz. = 1 cent more. So, 32 oz. = .05 + .30 = .35.

44. (5,y) represents the sixth point in this sequence. Thus, the corresponding y value = (2)(6) = 12

45. Let x = smaller number, 2.5x = larger number.

Then, $\dfrac{X}{2.5X} = \dfrac{1}{2.5} = \dfrac{10}{25} = \dfrac{2}{5}$

46. $12 - $3.75 = $8.25. Then, $8.25 ÷ .75 = 11 weeks

47. Radius = 10 in. Area = (3.14)(10^2) = 314 sq.in.

48. .045 = 4.5%

49. $\dfrac{20}{50} = 40\%$

50. (225%) (160) = (2.25) (160) = 360

ARITHMETICAL REASONING
EXAMINATION SECTION
TEST 1

DIRECTIONS: Each question or incomplete statement is followed by several suggested answers or completions. Select the one that BEST answers the question or completes the statement. *PRINT THE LETTER OF THE CORRECT ANSWER IN THE SPACE AT THE RIGHT.*

1. On January 1, a family was receiving supplementary monthly public assistance of $280 for food, $240 for rent, and $140 for other necessities. In the spring, their rent rose by 10%, and their rent allotment was adjusted accordingly. In the summer, due to the death of a family member, their allotments for food and other necessities were reduced by 1/7. Their monthly allowance check in the fall should be

    A. $624   B. $644   C. $664   D. $684

2. Twice a month, a certain family receives a $340 general allowance for rent, food, and clothing expenses. In addition, the family receives a specific supplementary allotment for utilities of $384 a year, which is added to their semi-monthly check.
If the general allowance alone is reduced by 5%, what will be the TOTAL amount of their next semi-monthly check?

    A. $323   B. $339   C. $340   D. $355

3. If each supervising clerk in a certain unit sees an average of 9 clients in a 7-hour day and there are 15 supervising clerks in the unit, APPROXIMATELY how many clients will be seen in a 35-hour week?

    A. 315   B. 405   C. 675   D. 945

4. In one day, an aide receives 18 inquiries by phone and 27 inquiries in person. What percentage of the inquiries received that day were by phone?

    A. 33%   B. 40%   C. 45%   D. 60%

5. If the weekly paychecks for 5 employees are $258.64, $325.48, $287.34, $271.50, and $313.12, then the combined weekly income for the 5 employees is

    A. $1,455.68   B. $1,456.08   C. $1,461.68   D. $1,474.08

6. Suppose that there are 17 aides working in an office where many community complaints are received by telephone. In one ten-day period, 4,250 calls were received.
If the same number of calls were received each day, and the aides divided the work load equally, about how many calls did each aide respond to daily?

    A. 25   B. 35   C. 75   D. 250

7. Suppose that an assignment was divided among 5 aides. If the first aide spent 67 hours on the assignment, the second aide spent 95 hours, the third aide spent 52 hours, the fourth aide spent 78 hours, and the fifth aide spent 103 hours, what was the AVERAGE amount of time spent by each aide on the assignment?
_______ hours.

    A. 71   B. 75   C. 79   D. 83

8. If there are 240 employees in a center and 1/3 are absent on the day of a bad snow-storm, how many employees were at work in the center on that day?

   A. 80   B. 120   C. 160   D. 200

9. Suppose that an aide takes 25 minutes to prepare a letter to a client.
If the aide is assigned to prepare 9 letters on a certain day, how much time should she set aside for this task? _______ hours.

   A. 3 3/4   B. 4 1/4   C. 4 3/4   D. 5 1/4

10. Suppose that a certain center uses both Form A and Form B in the course of its daily work and that Form A is used 4 times as often as Form B.
If the total number of both forms used in one week is 750, how many times was Form A used?

   A. 100   B. 200   C. 400   D. 600

11. Suppose a center has a budget of $2,185.40 from which 8 desks costing $156.10 apiece must be bought.
How many additional desks can be ordered from this budget after the 8 desks have been purchased?

   A. 4   B. 6   C. 9   D. 14

12. When researching a particular case, a team of 16 aides was asked to check through 234 folders to obtain the necessary information.
If half the aides worked twice as fast as the other half, and the slow group checked through 12 folders each hour, about how long would it take to complete the assignment? _______ hours.

   A. 4 1/4   B. 5   C. 6   D. 6 1/2

13. The difference in the cost of two typewriters is $56.64. If the less expensive typewriter costs $307.22, what is the cost of the other typewriter?

   A. $343.86   B. $344.06   C. $363.86   D. $364.06

14. At the start of a year, a family was receiving a public assistance grant of $382 twice a month, on the 1st and 15th of each month. On March 1, their rent allowance was decreased from $150 to $142 a month since they had moved to a smaller apartment. On August 1, their semi-monthly food allowance, which had been $80.40, was raised by 10%. In that year, the TOTAL amount of money disbursed to this family was

   A. $4,544.20   B. $6,581.40   C. $9,088.40   D. $9,168.40

15. It is discovered that a client has received double public assistance for 2 months by hav-ing been enrolled at two service centers of the Department of Social Services.
The client should have received $168 twice a month instead of the double amount. He now agrees to repay the money by equal deductions from his public assistance check over a period of 12 months. What will the amount of his NEXT check be?

   A. $112   B. $140   C. $154   D. $160

16. Suppose a study is being made of the composition of 3,550 families receiving public
assistance. Of the first 1,050 families reviewed, 18% had four or more children.
If, in the remaining number of families, the percentage with four or more children is half
as high as the percentage in the group already reviewed, then the percentage of families with four or more children in the entire group of families is MOST NEARLY

    A.   12   B.   14   C.   16   D.   27

17. Suppose that food prices have risen 13%, and an increase of the same amount has been
granted in the food allotment given to people receiving public assistance.
If a family has been receiving $810 a month, 35% of which is allotted for food, then the
TOTAL amount of public assistance this family receives per month will be changed to

    A. $805.42   B. $840.06   C. $846.86   D. $899.42

18. Assume that the food allowance is to be raised 5% in August but will be retroactive for
four months to April.
The retroactive allowance is to be divided into equal sections and added to the public
assistance checks for August, September, October, November, and December. A family which has been receiving $840 monthly, 40% of which was allotted for food, will
receive what size check in August?

    A. $853.44   B. $856.80   C. $861.00   D. $870.24

19. A blind client, who receives $210 public assistance twice a month, inherits 14 shares of
stock worth $180 each.
The client is required to sell the stock and spend his inheritance before receiving more
public assistance. Using his public assistance allowance as a guide, how many months
are his new assets expected to last?

    A.   6   B.   7   C.   8   D.   12

20. The Department of Social Services has 16 service centers. These centers may be
divided into those which are downtown and those which are uptown. Two of the centers
are special service centers and are downtown, while the remainder of the centers are
general service centers. There is a total of 7 service centers downtown.
The percentage of the general service centers which are uptown is MOST NEARLY

    A.   56   B.   64   C.   69   D.   79

21. For six months, a family lived in a 4-room apartment where they paid $380 a month. They
made an intrasite move to a 4-room apartment where they paid $85 per room a month for
six months.
Comparing the two six-month periods, the TOTAL amount of money the family saved
by making the intrasite move was

    A. $240   B. $290   C. $430   D. $590

22. To calculate a tenant's usable income, you should make Social Security deductions of
4.4 percent on salary up to a maximum of $9,000 and State Disability deductions of .5
percent on salary up to $3,000.
What does a tenant's combined deduction amount to if his annual salary is $13,400?

    A. $411.00   B. $568.60   C. $619.60   D. $700.00

23. If the temporary relocation expenses for housing are set at $18 per day for one adult and $10 per day for each additional person in a room, how much money is allowed for a woman and four children temporarily relocated in one room for a period of six days?   23._____

    A. $168   B. $348   C. $378   D. $518

24. According to relocation policy, a family relocating to private housing from federally-aided or certain other sites will be granted a relocation payment. This payment equals the difference between 1/5 of the family's yearly income and the scheduled yearly rent for a standard apartment for their size family.   24._____
    Suppose a 2-person family whose yearly income is $12,900 has been unable to obtain public housing and so finds a one-bedroom private apartment. The scheduled rent for a one-bedroom apartment appropriate for their occupancy is $240 a month. What payment will they receive?

    A. $240   B. $288   C. $300   D. $410

25. A family on a housing relocation site is paying $410 per month for rent. This represents 25% of their gross monthly income.   25._____
    If the husband earns 4/5 of their total combined monthly income, how much does the wife earn per month?

    A. $328   B. $540   C. $1,280   D. $1,600

KEY (CORRECT ANSWERS)

1.	A	11.	B
2.	B	12.	D
3.	C	13.	C
4.	B	14.	D
5.	B	15.	B
6.	A	16.	A
7.	C	17.	C
8.	C	18.	D
9.	A	19.	A
10.	D	20.	B

21.	A
22.	A
23.	B
24.	C
25.	A

SOLUTIONS TO PROBLEMS

1. After spring, the rent allotment should be $(240+24) = $264 After the summer, the reduced allotment for food and other necessities should be $[(280+140)-1/7(280+140)] = $[(420 - 1/7(420)] = $(420-60) = $360. ∴ The monthly check in the fall including rent, food, and other necessities should be $360 + $264 = $624

2. Amount of general allowance in the family's semi-monthly check = $340. Amount of utilities allotment in the family's semi-monthly check: $$\left(\frac{384}{12} \times \frac{1}{2}\right) = \$16$$ Amount of general allowance in family's semi-monthly check after a 5% reduction = $340 less 5% of $340 = $(340-17) = $323 Total amount of the next month's semi-monthly check: Reduced general allowance + utilities allotment = $323 + $16 = $339

3. During 7 hours, a total of (15)(9) = 135 clients can be seen. Thus, in 35 hours, a total of (135)(5) = 675 clients will be seen.

4. 18/(18+27) = .40 = 40%

5. $258.64 + $325.48 + $287.34 + $271.50 + $313.12 = $1456.08

6. 4250 / 10 = 425 calls per day. Then, 425 / 17 = 25

7. (67+95+52+78+103) / 5 = 79 hours

8. Number present = (240)(2/3) = 160

9. (25)(9) = 225 min. = 3 hrs. 45 min. = 3 3/4 hrs.

10. Let x, 1/4x = number of forms A, B, respectively. Then, x + 1/4 x = 750. Solving, x = 600

11. $2185.40 - (8)($156.10) = $936.60. Then, $936.60 v 156.10 = 6 desks

12. Since the slow group did 12 folders each hour, the faster group did 24 folders each hour. Then, 234 / (12+24) = 6 1/2 hrs.

13. Expensive typewriter costs $307.22 + $56.64 = $363.86

14. For months of January and February, the amount the family receives is $(382x2x2) = $1528
    For months of March through July, the family receives $(764-8) x 5 = $3780
    For months of August through December, the family receives $(756+16.08) x 5 = $3860.40 The total amount of money disbursed to this family is $1528 + $3780 + $3860.40 = $9,168.40

15. The overpayment for 2 months = ($168)(4) = $672. If this is paid back over 12 months, each month's amount is reduced by $672 / 12 = $56. Then, each check (semi-monthly) is reduced by $28. His next check will be $168 - $28 = $140

16. (1050)(.18) + (2500)(.09) = 414. Then, 414 / 3550 = 12%

17. ($810)(.35) = $283.50 originally allotted for food. The new food allotment = ($283.50)(1.13) = $320.355. The total assistance now = $810 - $283.50 + $320.355 = $846.855 or $846.86

18. ($840)(.40) = $336 per month for food. The new food allowance = ($336)(1.05) = $352.80 per month. The difference of $16.80 is retroactive to April, which means ($16.80)(9) = $151.20 additional money for August through December. Each check for these 5 months will be increased by $15.20 / 5 = 30.24. Thus, the check in August = $840 + 30.24 = $870.24

19. ($180)(14) = $2520. Then, $2520 / $420 = 6 months

20. 5 general are -downtown; ... 9 of 14 general are uptown; 9 / 14 $\approx$ 64%.

21. ($85)(4) = $340 per month. Savings per month = $380 - $340 = $40 For six months, the savings = $240

22. ($9000)(.044) + ($3000)(.005) = $411 total deductions

23. ($18+$40)(6) = $348 relocation expenses

24. ($240)(12) - (1/5)($12,900) = $300 relocation payment

25. $410 ÷ .25 = $1640. The wife earns (1640)(1/5) = $328 each month.

TEST 2

 Each question or incomplete statement is followed by several suggested answers or completions. Select the one that BEST answers the question or completes the statement. *PRINT THE LETTER OF THE CORRECT ANSWER IN THE SPACE AT THE RIGHT.*

1. A project tenant who owns and drives a taxicab for a living, reports for a three-month period, an income of $6,250 after operating expenses of $1,300 have been considered. In addition, his tips are valued at 12% of his income before operating expenses. An estimate of his yearly income is MOST NEARLY

    A. $22,000   B. $23,000   C. $28,000
    D. $28,500   E. $29,000

2. The maximum annual subsidy which can be paid by the State toward the operation of any low-rent housing project is the sum of the annual interest on the total original loan for building the project and 1% of the portion of the loan actually spent. If the original loan for a project was $8,000,000 at 1 3/4% interest, but only $7,500,000 was actually spent, then the MAXIMUM annual subsidy is

    A. $140,000   B. $145,000   C. $215,000
    D. $220,000   E. 271,250

3. In 2003, the cost of repairs and maintenance at a certain housing project was $5,589 more than in 2002, representing an increase of 4.6%. A further increase at the same rate was anticipated for 2004. The cost of repairs and maintenance in 2004 was MOST NEARLY

    A. $127,100
    B. $132,700
    C. $132,900
    D. $133,000
    E. an amount which cannot be determined from the given data

4. Each day a delivery truck used by the Housing Authority travels 25 miles from a project to a storehouse and 25 miles on the return trip. It travels at the rate of 30 miles per hour going to the storehouse and at the rate of 20 miles per hour returning. The average rate, in miles per hour, for the roundtrip is MOST NEARLY

    A. 24
    B. 25
    C. 26
    D. the square root of 600
    E. an amount which cannot be determined from the given data 0

5. A report on the first 6,000 applications for apartments in a certain project containing 1,400 apartments indicated that those who were ineligible fell into four categories: 2,800 ineligible for reason A, 600 ineligible for reason B, 1,200 ineligible for reason C, and 400 ineligible for reason D. If the same proportions continue for the remaining 21,500 applications, then the percentage of eligible applicants who can be given apartments in the project is MOST NEARLY

    A. 25   B. 30   C. 33   D. 40   E. 60

6. The number of applications for apartments in low-rent housing projects was 40,000 in 1999. The number of applications increased 5% in 2000, and increased again in 2001 by 6% over the 2000 total.
The percentage by which the 2001 figures exceed the 1999 figures is

   A. 5.3   B. 6.0   C. 11.0   D. 11.3   E. 30.0

6.____

7. A rectangular lot, 75 feet by 11.0 feet, was purchased as part of a project site for $28,500.
The price per square foot of this lot is MOST NEARLY

   A. $2.85   B. $3.45   C. $3.95   D. $30.00   E. $30.95

7.____

8. It has been estimated that 125 kilowatt-hours of electricity are used each month in one average Housing Authority apartment at a cost of 14.8 cents per kilowatt-hour.
On this basis, the total cost of the electricity used in one year in a project containing 1,400 apartments is MOST NEARLY

   A. $20,000   B. $25,000   C. $200,000
   D. $250,000   E. $2,000,000

8.____

9. The walls and ceilings of 20 rooms are to be painted with the same kind of paint, each room being 15 feet long, 12 feet wide, and 10 feet high. Each room contains two windows, each 3 feet by 6 feet, and a door 3 feet by 8 feet, which are not to be painted. One gallon of paint covers 400 square feet of surface.
The number of gallons of paint needed is MOST NEARLY

   A. 33   B. 34   C. 35   D. 36   E. 75

9.____

10. A group of buildings is valued at $11,500,000. Assume that the cost of fire insurance for these buildings is 5.3 cents per $100 of valuation per year.
The cost of fire insurance for one year is MOST NEARLY

   A. $600   B. $6,000   C. $20,000
   D. $60,000   E. $2,000,000

10.____

11. Of the 15 employees in a certain unit, one-third earn $27,600 per year, three earn $32,600, one earns $46,400, and the rest earn $33,800.
The average salary of the employees of this unit is MOST NEARLY

   A. $31,000   B. $32,000   C. $33,000   D. $34,000   E. $35,000

11.____

12. Four pieces, each 2'5 3/8" long, are cut from a piece of pipe 16 1/2' long.
The length of the remaining piece of pipe is

   A. 6'8 1/2"   B. 6'10"   C. 6'10 3/8"
   D. 6'11 1/8"   E. 9'9 1/2"

12.____

13. A tenant earns E dollars a month, spends S dollars a week, and saves the rest.
The tenant's yearly savings can be expressed by

   A. 12(E-4S)   B. 12E - 52S   C. 12(E-S)
   D. 52(E-4S)   E. E - S

13.____

14. A unit of fifteen Housing Assistants has been assigned the job of interviewing applicants.   14.____
Each interview takes 35 minutes, and an additional 10 minutes is needed for making
entries and notes. The last interview each day is always scheduled so that it can be completed that day.
The number of applicants who can be interviewed in a week, consisting of five 7-hour
days, is MOST NEARLY

    A.   375   B.   525   C.   675   D.   700   E.   725

15. A review of the 14,000 applications for apartments in a certain project containing 1,200   15.____
apartments indicated that 4,800 applicants were eligible and 6,400 were ineligible. No
decision could be reached on the remaining applications because certain necessary
information was omitted by the applicants, but it was assumed that the proportion of eligible and ineligible applicants would remain the same as in those already decided.
On the basis of these figures, the percentage of eligible applicants who can be given
apartments in the project is

    A.   under 17%   B.   17%   C.   20%
    D.   25%   E.   33 1/3%

16. An oil burner in a housing development burns 76 gallons of fuel oil per hour. At 9 A.M. on   16.____
a very cold day, the superintendent asks the Housing Manager to put in an emergency
order for more fuel oil. At that time, he reports that he has on hand 266 gallons. At noon,
he again comes to the manager, notifying him that no oil has been delivered.
The MAXIMUM amount of time that he can continue to furnish heat without receiving
more oil is

    A.   no more time   B.   1/2 hour   C.   1 hour
    D.   1 1/2 hours   E.   2 hours

17. As a result of reports received by the Housing Authority concerning the reputed ineligibil-   17.____
ity of 756 tenants because of above-standard incomes, an intensive check of their
employers has been ordered. Four housing assistants have been assigned to this task.
At the end of 6 days at 7 hours each, they have checked on 336 tenants. In order to
speed up the investigation, two more housing assistants are assigned to this point.
If they worked at the same rate, the number of additional 7-hour days it would take to
complete the job is MOST NEARLY

    A.   1   B.   3   C.   5   D.   7   E.   9

18. A municipal aide on a special trip is returning to his office from a point 17 1/2 miles away,   18.____
and makes the return trip to his office at an average speed of 25 miles an hour, except for
a 15-minute stopover at one point to get a flat tire fixed.
The time it should take him to reach his office is MOST NEARLY ______ minutes.

    A.   12   B.   22   C.   36   D.   42   E.   57

19. A district office has an assigned staff of 320 employees. Of this number, 25% are not   19.____
available for duty due to illness, vacations, and other reasons. Of those who are available
for duty, 1/8 are assigned to auditing and special projects, and the rest to handling the
workload. The ACTUAL number of employees available for handling the workload is

    A.   350   B.   310   C.   270   D.   210   E.   180

20. Two dozen shuttlecocks and four badminton rackets are to be purchased for a playground. The shuttlecocks are priced at $3.60 each, and the rackets at $27.50 each. The playground receives a discount of 30% from these prices. The TOTAL cost of this equipment is

    A. $72.90   B. $114.30   C. $13.7.48   D. $186.00   E. $220.70

20.____

21. On January 1, a family was receiving a public assistance allowance of $185 for food, $53 for clothing, $17.50 for utilities, and $22 for personal needs, all semi-monthly, and a monthly allowance of $550 for rent. On May 1, the rent allowance was increased by 12% but all other allowances remained the same for the rest of the year.
The TOTAL amount of money granted this family during the year was

    A. $10,528   B. $13,262   C. $13,788
    D. $21,056   E. $27,676

21.____

22. It has been decided to make changes in food allotments to clients receiving public assistance to conform to changes in food costs. Of the food allowance, 30% is intended for meat, 30% for fruits and vegetables, 25% for groceries, and 15% for dairy products. Assume that meat prices have gone up 10%, fruit and vegetable prices have gone down 20%, grocery prices have gone up 5%, and dairy prices have remained the same. For a family that has been receiving $400 per month for food, the new monthly food allowance will be

    A. $333   B. $375   C. $393   D. $403.50   E. $420

22.____

23. On January 1, a family was receiving a public assistance allowance of $195 for food, $63 for clothing, $27.50 for utilities, and $32 for personal needs, all semi-monthly, and a monthly allowance of $510 for rent. On June 1, the rent allowance was increased by 12%, but all other allowances remained the same for the rest of the year.
The TOTAL amount of money granted this family during the year was

    A. $13,843.40   B. $14,107.20   C. $14,168.40
    D. $14,474.40   E. $16,886.80

23.____

24. A member of a family receiving public assistance amounting to $600 monthly has obtained a part-time job, for which he is paid $40 a day. He is employed 3 days a week. His carfare costs $3.00 per day and his lunches $2.00 per day. Assume that there are 4 1/3 weeks per month. The Department of Welfare requires that net earnings be deducted from relief allowances.
The family's semi-monthly public assistance allowance should be reduced to

    A. $40.00   B. $72.50   C. $96.25   D. $123.75   E. $145.00

24.____

25. A couple living in a furnished room has been receiving a public assistance grant of $375 semi-monthly and has been paying a weekly rent of $75. The landlord has been granted a 12% increase in rent. Assume that a month consists of 4 1/3 weeks.
The amount of the new semi-monthly grant, including this rent increase, that the couple will receive will be MOST NEARLY

    A. $394.50   B. $397   C. $409   D. $514   E. $557

25.____

KEY (CORRECT ANSWERS)

1.	D		11.	B
1.	C		12.	A
2.	C		13.	B
3.	A		14.	C
4.	B		15.	C
5.				
6.	D		16.	B
7.	B		17.	C
8.	D		18.	E
9.	A		19.	D
10.	B		20.	C

21.	C
22.	C
23.	C
24.	B
25.	A

———

SOLUTIONS TO PROBLEMS

1. For 3 months, income = $6250 + (.12)($7550) = $7156 Then, annual income = ($7154)(4) = $28,624, closest to $28,500

2. Maximum annual subsidy = ($8,000,000)(.0175) + (.01)($7,500,000) = $215,000

3. Cost in 2002 = $5589 / .046 = $121,500. The cost in 2003 = $121,500 + $5589 = $127,089. This means the cost in 2004 = ($127,089)(1.046) = $132,900

4. Average rate = total distance / total time = (25+25) ÷ (25/30 + 25/20) = 24 mph.

5. Out of 6000, number of eligible = 6000 - 2800 - 600 - 1200 - 400 = 1000. Thus, for 27,500 applications, (1/6)(27,500) = 4583 would be eligible. Finally, 1400 ÷ 4583 ≈ 30%

6. Number of applications in 2000 = (40,000)(1.05) = 42,000 Number of applications in 2001 = (42,000)(1.06) = 44,520 Then, (44,520-40,000) ÷ 40,000 = 11.3%

7. $28,500 ÷ [(75X110)] = $3.45 per sq.ft.

8. Total cost = (125)(.148)(12)(1400) = $310,800; closest to choice D of $250,000

9. Painted area of each room = (2)(15)(10) + (2)(12)(10) + (15)(12) - (2)(3)(6) - (3)(8) = 660 sq.ft. So, (20)(660) = 13,200 sq.ft. to be painted in all rooms. Finally, 13,200 / 400 = 33 gallons of paint needed

10. Insurance cost = (.053)($11,500,000)/$100 = $6095, closest to $6000

11. [(5)($27,600)+(3)($32,600)+(1)(46,400)+(6)($33,800)]/15 = $32,333, closest to $32,000

12. 16 1/2 - (4)(2'5 3/8") = 16'6" - 8'21 1/2" = 16'6" - 9'9 1/2" = 6'8 1/2"

13. Annual savings = 12E - 52S

14. $7 \div \dfrac{3}{4} = 9.\overline{3}$, which means each interviewer can interview a maximum of 9 applicants each day. Then, (5)(9)(15) = 675 applicants.

15. 4800/(4800+6400) = 3/7 eligible. On that assumption, there would be (3/7)(14,000) = 6000 eligible applicants. Then, 1200/6000 = 20%

16. 266 - (3)(76) = 38 gallons of oil left. Then, 38 / 76 =1/2 hour

17. (6)(7)(4) = 168 hrs. to check on 336 tenants. This means 2 tenants require 1 man-hour. Now, (6)(7)(x days) = man-hrs. would be needed to check the remaining 420 tenants. This requires 210 man-hours. So, (6)(7)(x) = 210. Solving, x = 5

18. $\dfrac{17.5}{25}$ = .7 hr. = 42 min. Total time = 42 + 15 = 57 min.

19. Number available = 320[1-.25-(1/8)(.75)] = 210

20. Total cost = (.70)[(24)($3.60)+(4)(27.50)] = $137.48

21. From January through April, amount = (8)($185+$53+$17,50+$22) + (4)($550) = $4420.
From May through December, amount = (16)($185+$53+$17.50+$22) + (8)($550)(1.12)
= $9368 Total annual amount = $4420 + $9368 = $13,788

22. Meat allowance = ($400)(.30)(1.10) = $132; fruit and vegetable allowance =
($400)(.3O)(.80) = $96; grocery allowance = ($400)(.25)(1.05) = $105; dairy allowance =
($400)(,15) = $60 New monthly allowance = $132 + $96 + $105 + $.60 = $393

23. From January through May, amount = (10)($195+$63+$27.50+$32) + (5)($510) = $5725.
From June through December, amount = (14)($195+$63+$27.50+$32) + (7)($510)(1.12)
= $8443.40. Total annual amount = $5725 + $8443.40 = $14,168.40

24. Monthly assistance should be reduced to $600 - [(40)(3)(4 1/3) - ($5)(3)(4 1/3)] = $145.
So, the semi-monthly amount is now $145 / 2 = $72.50

25. ($75) (4 1/3) / 2 = $162.50 = original semi-monthly rent.
New semi-monthly rent = (162.50)(1.12) = $182. Since this represents an increase of
$19.50, the new semi-monthly grant will be increased to $375 + $19.50 = $394.50

9 781731 808646